S0-AKG-106

A WINTER IN THE SUN
THE PLEASURES (AND A FEW PITFALLS)
OF THE CARIBBEAN CRUISING
LIFESTYLE

BOOKS BY BILL ROBINSON

The Science of Sailing
New Boat
A Berth to Bermuda
Where the Trade Winds Blow
Expert Sailing
Over the Horizon
The World of Yachting
The Best from Yachting (editor)
Better Sailing for Boys and Girls
The America's Cup Races (co-author)
Legendary Yachts
The Sailing Life
The Right Boat for You
Great American Yacht Designers
America's Sailing Book
A Sailor's Tales
Cruising: The Boats and the Places
South to the Caribbean
Where to Cruise
Islands
Caribbean Cruising Handbook
Eighty Years of Yachting
Cruising the Easy Way
Best Sailing Spots Worldwide
Destruction at Noonday
The Sailing Mystique

* published by Sheridan House

A WINTER IN THE SUN
THE PLEASURES (AND A FEW PITFALLS)
OF THE CARIBBEAN CRUISING
LIFESTYLE

BILL ROBINSON

SHERIDAN HOUSE

First published 1995 by
Sheridan House Inc.
145 Palisade Street
Dobbs Ferry, NY 10522

Copyright © 1995 by Bill Robinson

All rights reserved. No part of this publication may be reproduced, stored in a
retrieval system or transmitted in any form or by any means, electronic,
mechanical, photocopying, recording, or otherwise, without the prior
permission in writing of Sheridan House.

Library of Congress Cataloging-in-Publication Data

Robinson, Bill, 1918–
    A winter in the sun : the pleasures (and a few pitfalls) of the Caribbean
cruising lifestyle / Bill Robinson.
        p. cm.
    ISBN 0–924486–69–4 : $17.95
    1. Leeward Islands (West Indies)—Description and travel. 2. Yachts and
yachting—Leeward Islands (West Indies). 3. Sailing—Leeward Islands (West
Indies). 4. Brunelle (Boat). 5. Robinson, Bill, 1918– —Journeys—Leeward
Islands (West Indies). 6. Caribbean Area—Description and Travel. I. Title.
F2006.R63 1995
917.29704—dc20   94–44860
                                                                          CIP

Design by Sarah K. Myers

Photos by the author

Printed in the United States of America

ISBN 0–924486–69–4

CONTENTS

PREFACE

LOOKING BACK OVER a lifetime of cruising, reading through my logs, and deep in the enjoyment of re-living the many marvelous memories, I wanted to share some experiences that would typify what a cruising lifestyle has meant for my wife Jane and me, and that would serve as a guide for those who are interested in this form of the pursuit of happiness.

My involvement with cruising started in 1932 and has been a major element in my life ever since. While cotton has given way to Dacron and Kevlar, mahogany to fiberglass, and spruce to aluminum, the verities are still very much there. The basics of cruising pleasure in 1932, 1938, and 1961, 1980 or the '90s are the same. The sea, the sky, and the wind remain; while some cruising areas have undergone major changes under the pressure of increased popularity, there are many good ones there for the enjoyment.

Of the many areas Jane and I have sampled worldwide, the Caribbean remains a constant as the one that best combines the pleasures, challenges and availability. We have come to know it well, basing our boats there for over a dozen years, while also sailing in borrowed boats and charters. For us, and for many, many enthusiasts, it embodies the ultimate ideal in cruising. What we have learned from these past experiences makes today's continuing pleasures all the more meaningful, and I have gone over my logs to pick the most typical of times that combine these elements. The winter in the sun that seemed to work best for this purpose was 1980–81, though the year digits could be switched backward to early days or forward to today with very little basic change. That winter season covered a good range of Caribbean highlights, from the U.S. and British Virgins to St. Martin and Antigua, and the passages between them. Fortunately I did keep the logs, and, between deciphering my handwriting and figuring out some saltsplotched entries, along with the occasional poser of trying to remember just who good old Sally and Joe were who came aboard for a drink in Village Cay, it all came together. By sharing this with you, the reader, the details of how we did it will, I hope, become a "how-to" for those who would like to try something similar, or at least dream about "someday," and a standard of comparison for sailors already experienced in this kind of operation.

The sailing conditions that Columbus and Sir Francis Drake knew are still the basics of this enjoyment, and the passages we made and the harbors and islands we visited still serve as a guide to this rewarding experience. For me, it is rewarding, in re-living our adventures, to share them with you.

BILL ROBINSON
RUMSON, N.J.

I

ANTICIPATION

ELBOWING OUR WAY through the steaming shambles of the San Juan Airport, past extended families of locals blocking the passageways in emotional reunions, we conquered the tortuous route to the departure gate for Beef Island to find that, as usual, the shuttle plane was delayed. At least we had our luggage, which from rueful past experiences we had learned to take care of personally. The waiting room was semi-air-conditioned, but, in getting off the plane from Newark and in passing through the open areas of the terminal, with our December-oriented New Jersey constitutions, Jane and I had been smothered in the warmly all-encompassing welcome of Puerto Rico's humidity.

We sat in the departure waiting room with sweat trickling down inside our travel clothes, surrounded by fellow passengers-to-be, most of whom were obviously rigged to go sailing. There were a few British Virgin Islanders, sedate in more formal attire, resigned and complacent in contrast to the nervous expectancy of the northern visitors. Eventually an announcement in Spanish, useless to an all-English-speaking group, alerted us to progress, followed in Hispanic-accented English telling us they were ready to take us to Beef Island. That brought us to our feet.

Out on the broiling tarmac, where the sun's assault raised steam from pavement recently splashed by a shower, we shuffled to the good old DC–3 that awaited us, collecting heat, and gradually settled the confusion of taking seats. One more leg and we would be back to sailing country.

After we took off, with the rattle and rumble that only a DC–3 can generate, anticipation was increased by the glimpse below of deep blue rollers charging their white-capped way on the tradewinds from Africa toward Luquillo Beach's necklace of surf and sand. This contrasted with

I

the bulk inland of El Yunque, the rainmaker mountain, in its usual shroud of cumulus squalls. Then came the glittery spread of marinas, hotels and towering condos at Fajardo, which had been an isolated fishing village when I first saw it in the '50s. Puerto Rico dropped away, and Culebra's coves and deeply indented hurricane hole, Ensenada Honda, flashed by, reminders of intriguing explorations when we sailed through there in 1979.

Then off to starboard, St. Thomas's peaks, pock-marked everywhere with the white dots of houses, were higher than our altitude. They were followed by the lovely green hills of St. John's untouched national park. The plane's roar changed pitch and we began to lose altitude as Tortola's Mt. Sage, tallest in all the Virgins at about 1800 feet, loomed over us to port. Now we were getting close, and as usual, I tried to spot *Brunelle* in her berth at Road Town's Village Cay Marina, but we were beyond it before I could focus. I knew she was there, though, waiting for us, as we swooped downward over East End and bounced a bit on the Beef Island runway, which runs west-east to take care of 95 percent of the wind direction to be met.

Stepping off the plane into the slanting sun of late afternoon, I breathed deeply. This air had an entirely different feel to it from the humid oppression at San Juan. A fresh easterly trade riffled in across Trellis Bay, just off the end of the runway, where the aluminum masts of boats at anchor shone above the fringing palms. This was it. This was sailing country. We were back, and my walk became livelier as we were led across to the Arrivals area.

Queued up at the Immigration Desk, we had the first of the many greetings that always make us feel at home in the BVI, from the official, Mrs. Smith, in her badge and uniform of crisp white shirt and black skirt. She always remembers us and takes a moment to look through our passports to check on the previous times she had stamped and signed our entry, smiling shyly and handing them to us with a soft "Welcome back."

Baggage collected from the hustle and shambles of the luggage counter, we got a friendly wave-through from the Customs man, who seemed to recognize our beat-up blue duffels, and we found Dougie among the gaggle of cab drivers shouting for attention outside the Customs door. Stocky, with broad, smiling face rimmed with a fringe of beard, and a sailing hat jauntily on his head, he greeted us with a big grin, grabbed our bags and headed for his cab, a large Buick of uncertain age. He doubles as cab driver and caretaker of the sloop of a friend of ours, and we can usually single him out of the importuning mob. Sweeping out of the airport parking lot ahead of most of the flight's traffic, we were on our way the eight miles to Road Town in gathering twilight, which comes in as early as 1800 in December.

Dougie filled us in on recent weather; "not too much rain," and said that the season looked like a good one so far. Familiar landmarks flashed by as we crossed the tiny, one-lane Queen Elizabeth Bridge that connects Beef Island with Tortola, and continued on the bumpy road through the native settlement of East End, "patrolled" by "sleeping policemen," speed bumps in the road every few hundred yards. We bounced over them and onto the up-and-down hills of the coastal road, remembering again, after a moment of instinctive alarm, that we were in left-hand-driving country. Like all BVI taxi drivers, Dougie drives faster than we would choose, and it was a "grin and hang on" ride past the cluster of masts at Maya Cove, the fields of the Agricultural Station, practically the only level stretch on the ride, the swooping hills by the mangroves of Paraquita Cove, the island's best hurricane hole, and Brandywyne Bay. Several times, the road peaks out at the top of a curve, with Sir Francis Drake Channel directly below us and spread out in a shimmering panorama of sunset skies and distant islands. As often as we had done it, it was a breathtaking moment. We came down the last steep grade past the CSY Marina at Baugher's Bay on the east side of Road Harbour and curved around the head of the bay toward the civilization of Road Town.

When we came to the BVI on our first Caribbean bareboat cruise in 1966, all this area was mangrove swamp, and I remember standing at the bar of The Poop Deck, then the only gin mill in town, at the edge of the swamp, and listening to a not-very-sober customer pontificate about the future of the area. Sweeping his arm out to the east and northeast, and not enunciating very clearly, he said that the whole area would someday be all "roads, hotels, shops and marinas," and it was still a surprise to find that what I had taken for inebriated maunderings had come true.

Among the marinas in this "Phoenix of the Mangroves" was Village Cay, and that was where we hoped that *Brunelle* was ready for us. This would be a new experience, a new arrangement for us, simply cruising in an area with no "targets." There would be one or two commitments to certain events, covering for *Yachting* magazine, and we had a schedule of guests worked out for most of the winter. I looked forward to this new approach to cruising with hopes (and maybe a few doubts) about how it would work out. We had never spent such a long period on one of our boats without some ultimate goal at the end of the time. This was to be here and now, and it was a time of special anticipation.

3

2

WELCOME BACK

BRUNELLE WAS THERE, looking bright and clean. Peter Clarke, our new off-season boatkeeper, had her sparkling, in contrast to the previous year when we had had several days' work to put her in shape. There were only one or two glitches (there always has to be at least one) still to be solved, like a door latch and the hasp on one of the cockpit lockers. One of the more unpleasant encounters as part of coming back to her after a summer layup was missing: There didn't seem to be any cockroaches, in contrast to the army that had faced us the previous year. They do get aboard when a boat has been idle at a tropical pier for any length of time, but Peter had arranged for a fumigation service that had pretty well taken care of things. A carcass or two and a skitter here and there were minor worries.

Peter was there to greet us. A laid-back, soft-spoken South African, slender, blond and sunburned, he seemed as casual as the most carefree tourist, but he was a conscientious boatkeeper, who did his job well without fuss or flurry. The previous year, he had brought the dozen or so boats in his care in the marina safely through Hurricane David's crazily high tides, managing to get aboard each one, sometimes by swimming, to double up lines and check fenders. An excellent sailor himself, he is one of the top racing skippers at the BVI Yacht Club.

Over a beer, which he had made sure was frostily cold on the ice as a welcome aboard, he brought us up to date on the local scene and told one story on himself. Laughing in quiet embarrassment, he said, "I took *Brunelle* to the boatyard for her annual haulout in November, and I got very busy afterward doing other things. About a week later, Albie [Albie Stewart, manager of Tortola Yacht Services] called up and said, 'Peter, when are you coming for *Brunelle*? She's been ready for several days.'

4

"'Oh so that's where she is,' I said. 'I was wondering where she'd gotten to.'"

He did admit to a measure of absent-mindedness, but somehow it seemed to fit in with the BVI lifestyle.

In my own forgetfulness, I couldn't remember how to activate the cabin lights, a problem I'd also had the year before, but, after fumbling around for a while, it came back to me. Without bothering to unpack, we switched into sailing clothes that we kept on board, threw our duffels on the settee, and went ashore for dinner at Downstairs, the informal restaurant along the marina bulkhead.

Sipping our Mount Gay rum on the rocks, we looked out across the lights flickering on the water in the basin to *Brunelle*'s mast halfway out the pier, breathed a sigh, and almost audibly relaxed. So here we were, back for another season afloat, and the soft, harbor-scented tradewind, the lights dancing on the water, and the wonderful, gentle warmth were the promise of things to come. It would be our third season with *Brunelle*. We had sailed her down from the CSY builder's yard in Tampa in leisurely fashion in the spring of 1979, taking five months for the passage (written up in my 1982 book *South to the Caribbean*), and the previous winter we had taken her to St. Vincent and back.

Our original plan had been to circumnavigate the Caribbean, but we had given that up in St. Vincent the previous May and decided to base in the BVI due to a combination of circumstances. We had trouble confirming arrangements for leaving her in Venezuela for the summer, the drug situation in Colombia wiped out any thought of stopping there, and political problems and violence in Central America dampened enthusiasm for that part of the route. Also, we would have to have stalwart crew help, often hard to arrange, for the longer passages.

So, we had gone back to Tortola in eight hard-pressed days and had decided that this was the most sensible place for us to base. Jane and I were in our early 60s, and I was in an arrangement with the new owners of *Yachting* magazine (from which I had recently retired as Editor) which meant that I could sail as much as I wanted to and write columns and articles while doing it. My new title was Editor-at-Large. (Jane said it referred to my stomach, a not completely accurate canard; I only had a slight middle-aged spread, otherwise known as a pot belly.) These new developments had changed our focus from a definite plan and project to what might be more aptly called aimless pleasure, and we were looking forward to taking full advantage of it.

5

After the voyage down from Florida, we knew our limitations. Long sea passages with continued watchstanding would not be a good idea, even with extra hands. Most of our friends were in our age bracket and physical state, the next generation in our family was busily at work and only briefly available, and it would mean that we would have to proselytize younger strangers as crew, something we did not relish doing. Jane had had a heart attack and double bypass operation in 1976, and, while fully recovered, was not a candidate for strenuous passagemaking. While I was in perfect health, shoulders and knees were showing the effects of almost 50 years of playing squash, and I was not exactly gazelle-like in moving about on deck. Leisurely port-to-port cruising in the Eastern Caribbean was a much more sensible and manageable lifestyle. *Brunelle* was well set up for us to handle by ourselves in daytime cruising, and she was laid out properly for having another couple as guests, since she had two private cabins with heads.

Why did we choose this way to retire? Why not a winter home in Florida or the islands, or extended travel, now that we had the time? Some friends looked at us as slightly crazy with our plans to spend months at a time in the confines of a boat, taking on the uncertainties of weather, strange places, physical problems of our own and the boat, and separation from the "civilization" of comfortable living, family, friends, TV and easy shopping. These were admittedly concerns, but the balance came out strongly as a plus for our situation.

When I first retired, an already retired friend had given me that slightly cynical advice of "Don't go to the bank and the post office on the same day" as a solution for how to occupy yourself in this sudden surplus of freedom, when time would hang heavy, but I was not ready for that approach to life. Ever since the bug had bitten me at age 13 on a cruise to Martha's Vineyard and Nantucket when I was at summer camp Viking on Cape Cod, I had been a cruising addict, but my opportunities had been in small bites of a week or two, even though I had a lot more chances than most people through my job at *Yachting*. Now there was this almost limitless prospect, and I was not about to pass it up.

Considering all the cruising I had been able to do, it was ironic to look back at the summer of 1938 between my junior and senior years in college, when, instead of taking a summer job as a student-aid participant should, I chartered a 26-foot sloop and took off for the month of August for good old Nantucket and the Vineyard, thinking I would never have so much free time again. Little did I know, but now the free time was here.

6

Map of the Caribbean

Jane was willing to go along with my obsession. She was a good galley manager and enjoyed being aboard as a way of life. She had never been on a boat before we were married, but she had been brought up in a family that enjoyed outdoor life, and in the almost 40 years of our life together, understanding this general approach, she had learned the rudiments of sailing and was good on the helm, though she never considered herself an expert sailor. She did have one failing. Even though she could knit socks, sweaters, baby blankets and other complicated patterns while reading a book, watching TV, or standing on her head, she could never convince herself that she could tie a clove hitch or a bowline, and she would always wail "What's clockwise?" in a panic when trying to put a sheet on a winch. All in all though, she knew how to be a good shipmate, and our marital relations (in all phases) had really been enriched by the close association of being constantly together in these special circumstances for months at a time.

So we were settled into our new, take-it-easy situation, with no great projects of circumnavigating the world, or even the Caribbean, but there were still some questions. As far as leaving home and "civilization" behind, we did not want to live aboard full time. We loved our waterfront house on Rumson's Shrewsbury River, with the relaxed daysailing in our 18-foot Sanderling catboat, and the weather on the North Jersey Coast is generally quite pleasant from May into November, blessed by prevailing seabreezes and a consistently mild climate. It was only winter that we wanted to avoid. We had family and friends to enjoy, but, as will be seen, *Brunelle* was a big plus in those relationships. A winter afloat would be enough.

The question was often asked—why the Virgin Islands? Why not bring the boat north in the summer? Wouldn't it be easier to have her in Florida or the Bahamas? We would be foreigners in a strange land. Wouldn't that be awkward?

First of all, I did not want the north-south commutation. The Intracoastal Waterway has its charms, but it can also be a long-drawn-out chore to negotiate. We had seen enough of it to know both sides of operating there, and I did not want to spend the time it would take. As for the offshore passage back and forth, forget it. Even in our younger days this would have been more than we wanted to handle. I have never heard from a boat owner who has done this who had anything good to say about the experience. It was tough and rough and not for us.

In all our cruising in the most popular areas around the world, we had never found a place that combined better features than the BVI, at least for

The Baths at Virgin Gorda

present purposes. We had seen most of the glamour areas: Les Îles sous le Vent off Tahiti, Tonga, Fiji, Hawaii, the Barrier Reef of Australia, the Greek Isles, Sardinia-Corsica, the San Blas Islands, and of course the Bahamas and both coasts of Florida. They were all great cruising grounds, but not for use as a permanent base. Obviously the more remote ones were not practical, but none combined the easy accessibility (even with the good old shuttle from San Juan), the well-established facilities and services, the choice of good, close-together harbors, and the generally reliable weather of the BVI. Our past experiences there had made us feel completely at home—even the currency was U.S.—and I could think of no better place to base for the winter.

The British Virgins are not extensive. In an east-west stretch of less than 40 miles across Latitude 18°30′ North and between Longitudes 64° and 65° West, there are about 30 pieces of land big enough to be dignified by the term island. Then there is Anegada, off by itself 14 miles north of Virgin

9

Gorda, the easternmost of the BVI. The major islands are Jost Van Dyke, Tortola and Virgin Gorda, which have most of the population, numbering about 10,000 at the time we started basing there. The population has grown since then by more than half.

The area taken in by the U.S. and British Virgins was named by Columbus for the 10,000 virgins of Biblical lore. He was given to using Biblical references for the names of places he was "discovering," and he was impressed by this vast spread of islands looming purple on the horizon as he sailed by on his second voyage. From a few miles offshore, it is an awesome panorama of closely connected lumps and bumps.

The British sector of the Virgins is a colony of Great Britain, with a Governor-General representing the Crown, and a government that is locally self-operated, with a Chief Minister and a Legislative Council of BVI citizens, who go by the term of Belongers. Although originally settled in the 17th century by the Dutch, which accounts for such names as Jost Van Dyke, the islands have been British for most of their post-Columbian history, and they were not subjected to the continuing struggles between England, France, Holland, and Spain for control of other Caribbean territories in the 17th and 18th centuries. The pre-Columbian inhabitants were the peaceful Taino Indians of the Arawak tribe, as recent archeological digs have given confirming evidence. They eventually disappeared under the dual pressures of war with the fierce Caribs and European exploitation.

The population today is mainly descended from African slaves brought in during the 18th and early 19th centuries to work the sugar plantations that were the basis of the local economy. The islands were not as big or as well set up for sugar production as large ones like St. Kitts, Antigua, and St. Lucia, but there was prosperity from the trade, and a certain style of gracious living in the plantation manor house, supported by slavery.

There was also a cattle farming operation, with a reminder of it still existing in the name of Beef Island, Tortola's almost contiguous neighbor to the east, where the operation was based. There is a local legend that tells of the way the plantation owner, a woman, handled the problem of pirates, who were very active in the area, stealing her cattle. She politely invited them to a party at her estate, and when they were pleasantly inebriated and in a relaxed state, she had them all murdered by her staff. The foundations of her estate house are still visible on the slopes of Beef Island's impressive hump of a mountain.

When the British outlawed slavery in 1834, the sugar trade collapsed, and the BVI went into more than a century of sleepy oblivion. The freed slaves worked small farms as well as they could for subsistence living; there was some fishing and shipbuilding, and many locals turned to the sea for their trade. It was not until after World War II that the pressures of the modern world began to make themselves felt, and the big breakthrough in bringing the BVI into the mainstream, albeit in a very special way, was the establishment and growth of the charterboat industry in the '70s.

The inebriated prophet at the Poop Deck Bar in 1966 had been remarkably accurate in his predictions, and sleepy little Road Town, along the mangrove-lined bay, had developed quickly and remarkably. There were now more than 200 sailing yacht masts in a gleaming forest in the sunlight amid the new marinas, shops, restaurants, hotels, banks, and boatyards, and a poky backwater had become a vibrant center of the yachting world. We were glad to be a part of it.

As for the business of missing family and friends, they would be a major addition to our cruising pleasure as guests aboard. Shopping and general amenities were actually very civilized, and things like TV programs, with their deadly assault of ads about dandruff, gas pains, headache cures, sore feet, and breakfast cereals, had never loomed large in our routines. If we wanted to catch up with something like the Super Bowl or other such major events, there would always be a bar or hotel showing them.

And so we were here. Ordering conch fritters, our favorite local specialty, to add to our sense of place, we ate a relaxed dinner, thinking ahead to days to come, as the night breeze off the harbor wafted across the table.

3

BRUNELLE

BRUNELLE HAD WORKED out to be the ideal vessel for our new life. I have written her up in many other books and articles, but a short recap here might help to put her in focus. She was our third cruising boat, following a 24-foot Amphibi-Ette, *Mar Claro*, and an Out Island 36, *Tanagra*, both of which had worked out very well in their time and place, and which remain as very happy elements in our family sailing memories. For our Caribbean adventures we wanted something a bit bigger, sturdier, and more thoroughly thought-out for Caribbean cruising. *Brunelle*, named for a full-rigged ship out of Hull, England, that had been my grandfather's pride and joy to command, was a stock CSY 37, designed by Peter Schmitt for the Caribbean charter trade. She was 37'3" × 29' × 12' × 4'9". There was an alternate draft choice of six feet, but we had picked the shallower one to give us more gunkholing flexibility, and we were glad that we had. It did not seem to affect sailing qualities at all, and we did have a wider choice of operating, certainly in coming through the Bahamas, and also right here in the BVI. A description of her characteristics might serve as a general guide to what works and what doesn't work in cruising boats. Everyone has their own ideas and special requirements, but there are some basics that apply.

Although she was a stock boat, we did manage a few "custom" choices. First of all was the hull color. I had never taken to the standard CSY colors of what I called "baby-diaper-tan" topsides and a maroon cove stripe, and I talked the powers-that-be at CSY into giving us a pale blue topsides and dark blue stripe. Both *Mar Claro* and *Tanagra* had had this scheme, and it is a very fine combination of good looks and practicality. The blue is a "nautical" color that blends well with seascapes, and it is good for not showing stains easily. It is also cool enough for tropical use. The original

CSY 37 had been a dark green, but that would be impractical in the tropics, holding heat too readily. We also had ports installed from both the after cabin and the galley to the cockpit, which really helped with ventilation and communication. We also added something I had never thought much about—a gallows frame for the main boom, which was a joy in making sailhandling a lot easier. We had much better sails (from Ulmer) than the standard charterboat, and it was amazing to see what a difference they made in performance when we happened to be sailing near one of the boats from the charter fleet. To these we added a Flasher, Ulmer's name for a light-weight, poleless spinnaker that made much more fun out of downwind sailing. It had every color of the rainbow in its vertical stripes, and across the bottom, the horizontal stripes were orange and black for my college (Princeton) and blue and white for my prep school (Pingry). Speaking of prep, how preppy could you get—but it all made a striking sight when we broke it out, and always brought smiles.

The interior layout was fine, as I have said, for two couples, with a forward stateroom that had a full-sized comfortable bunk that could be two singles or a double, and a portside cabin aft with a settee that converted (after many contortions and a very special routine) into a double. Both cabins had their own head, and the only lapse in planning was that they were both on the port side. In passagemaking, it's always nice to have a head on each side, so the leeward one can be used for more comfortable sitting (and standing).

This layout was made possible by the engine installation, a Westerbeke 4–108 diesel, canted forward from its roomy position under the cockpit to a V-drive transmission under the companionway ladder. This allowed the full use of interior space without the engine being in the way, and the only drawback was that the transmission under the ladder was in a space so confined that an average husky male couldn't quite fit in there to work on it. When one had to, we would hear a series of strange moans, groans, and grunts as the work went on.

There was one odd new addition this year to the engineering department. When I turned the engine on for the first time, a thin stream of water came arching out of a tiny hole on the starboard side, just under the cockpit. My first reaction was that there was some weird leak, and then I remembered: On our journey south through the islands the previous winter, we had had a problem when water sucked up through the exhaust pipe, while we were sailing at hull-speed-plus on the port tack, and got into the cylinders. I didn't even know it was there, but there was an anti-siphoning valve at the top of an inverted U-bend in the pipe that was supposed to stop just such a thing from happening. It had frozen, and a new system, installed by Tortola Yacht Services during her haulout, sent a stream of water through the valve to keep it open. The thin stream made an odd-looking sight, and after the first surprise, we named it our Urinator.

Later on, a friend with a glossy 65-foot ketch saw me at a party and asked, "Bill, what's that little pisser you have?"

Thinking he was referring to *Brunelle*, which was, of course, just bigger than half the size of his boat, I was considerably insulted at what I took as a reference to my pride and joy, all 37 feet of her, and answered rather huffily, "She's a CSY 37."

It was his turn to be shocked, and then he laughed and said, "No. No. I just mean that stream of water that comes out of her topsides."

Ever after that, we would share a small laugh about how my little pisser was.

The galley was well laid-out to starboard of the companionway, with a sink and storage bin along the after bulkhead, and the propane stove and roomy mechanical refrigerator along the starboard side of the cabin. There was a good work space on top of the refrigerator, and forward of that was a settee that converted to an upper and lower berth. On the port side was a dinette, thankfully not a convertible one. I have smashed any number of toes and fingers, and uttered many oaths, in late-night attempts to convert a dinette to a bunk on boats that have had this arrangement, and we already had six good berths. Actually, we hardly ever used six bunks, except during visits from family and some very old friends who knew each other well.

The refrigerator operated by being run for an hour a day off a compressor attached to the main engine. The engine compartment also had a hot-water heater that worked off the engine or on shore power, and the propane tanks, protected by a carefully thought-out set of safety switches, were stored under the helmsman's seat all the way aft in the cockpit. (Some of my more humorous friends started calling it the "ejection seat.")

Topsides, she had a roomy, comfortable cockpit with a fitting on the binnacle for a portable table. People often forget how important cockpit comfort is, since 90 percent of waking hours are usually spent there. We ate all but a few of our meals in the cockpit, possible in the tropics if not in colder climates. A bimini over it, a good, strong one, was never lowered in our nine seasons aboard her in the tropics, as protection from the sun is absolutely vital. You eventually get used to craning your neck around it to look at the mainsail. Her main cabin area had a raised deck right out to the toerail, which makes for a bulkier profile, but adds all sorts of room below, where it is really needed to get a double-cabin aft-cockpit layout in 37 feet. It took some climbing to get over it and go forward, but there was a good flat space for dinghy stowage, and six hatches helped a lot with tropical demands on ventilation. The dinghy, incidentally, was a nine-foot Avon inflatable that served us well on two boats for 13 years with only minor repairs, and I could launch it and bring it aboard singlehanded, which was a great plus. I did not want an outboard because of maintenance and stowage problems (motor and gas). The dinghy's only drawback was that it wasn't the greatest rowboat, but we managed.

Finally, there was the rig, and I became a great fan of it. The mainsail, 365 square feet, had jiffy reefing that I could handle in a minute or two, and her headrig was a double one of a high-cut roller-furler jib, and a self-trimming staysail on a club. It was remarkable how much flexibility this combination had in adapting to varying wind conditions. In a full-sail breeze, the double jib setup was a good one to windward, probably not quite as good as a big genoa, but plenty good for cruising, and the combinations that could be achieved through reefing the main, and the choice of jibs, were remarkably effective. One trick we pulled repeatedly was simply to roll up the big jib at lunchtime so that she would ride remarkably level, and with satisfactory progress, under main and staysail. We dubbed this the "cocktail rig." And of course the roller-furling jib is the lazy cruising man's delight. Think of all the years we went without it!

There had to be something that was not perfect about her, and there were two small things. The forward ends of the raised deck jutted outboard, ending in a right angle, and this could cause embarrassing contact with pilings while making a landing. It would have been better if they had been rounded. Also, there were decorative trailboards on the bow that did not quite achieve the "classical" look that they were supposed to, and they once tore loose in heavy going in a rough head sea.

Small carpings about a vessel we had come to love, and as we had a post-prandial Mount Gay in the cockpit, we looked ahead eagerly to our season in the sun.

4

THE NEIGHBORHOOD

MEANWHILE, OF COURSE, we had to go to bed, and, if it had been a problem to remember how to activate the circuit for the cabin lights, that was nothing compared to trying to recollect the proper procedure for making up our double bunk from the daytime settee. I had gotten it down to a science the previous season, but the months away had clouded memory, and I had to start all over again.

We had to set it up each night and redo it as a settee each morning because it completely filled the space, making daytime use of the nav table, the VHF, and the electric switch panel really awkward if it remained as a bed. It was a perfectly good, roomy bunk when made up, with ventilation from a hatch above it, and ports high on the port bulkhead, and on the aft bulkhead giving on the cockpit. The head was just forward of it in its own cozy little compartment.

In all our years of marriage, Jane has always slept on my right. The other way round, I am sure that I'm in bed with a stranger, and I can't sleep at all. At home, we can each get out of our own side of the bed for nocturnal head visits, an almost standard activity in the advance toward geriatrics, but here, Jane's side was right against the bulkhead, and she had to climb over me to get out on my side, which almost inevitably would wake me up. Sometimes, in an attempt at gallantry, I would sit up, thinking to make it easier for her to slide across behind me, and we ended up meeting in mid-air.

We have tried it with me on the inside, but, in addition to the "stranger in my bed" syndrome, I usually manage to lean on Jane's hair or put an elbow in her solar plexus while making my move across, and we decided to stay with the conventional "bride-on-my-right" mode.

And so I went below, while Jane continued to sip her drink and contemplate the stars, and I sipped my drink and contemplated the system. Which did I do first? Put the bottom mattress on the deck while I flipped out the hinged board that filled in the double space? But then what did I do with the backrest, which would fall down before I could lift the board?

Finally, after fumbling a few false starts, with the backrest bouncing on my shoulders, I began to remember: Put the backrest on end against the cabin door in what amounted to a tiny entrance area, stand the bottom mattress up against the bulkhead, flip the hinged board into place, and then put the mattress halves down. Eureka, and I took a good swig of the drink. All that was left now was to crawl around on my hands and knees tucking the sheets in at the foot end aft, under the nav table. I didn't realize how ridiculous I could look doing this until, later in the cruise, I caught Jane and the guests peeking at me through the port and finally giving themselves away by bursting into giggles. Someone even took my picture doing it, featuring the rear end.

Bed was ready, and we settled into it with grateful sighs.

Because of the almost perpetual habit of the tradewind weather producing one-cloud rainsqualls now and then during the normal course of otherwise lovely weather, we had worked out a system of only leaving a hatch open that was directly over an occupied bunk. These could be shut quickly when the raindrops started to sprinkle on the face, instead of the awkward nuisance of dashing around the cabins in a half-awake panic. If we were at anchor, bow to wind, the side and aft ports could be left open, but they were sometimes on the windward side when we were in a marina slip, and it was amazing how quickly the atmosphere could become close with everything shut. Usually the squalls would spatter by in a matter of minutes.

There was only one light shower on this first night aboard, and we slept the sleep of weary travelers in a change of climate. We awoke in leisurely fashion at 0845 to a beautiful bright morning, with the perpetual little puffs of tradewind clouds shining in the sun as they wafted in from the east. This was the real thing. We were here.

Not having shopped yet, we went to Downstairs for breakfast, and the cheerful young waitress in her brown and tan uniform with swirling skirt, greeted us like long-lost friends. BV islanders tend to be shy and reserved at first, but once on familiar ground, they are very smiling and friendly. The orange juice, bacon, and eggs tasted awfully good as the breeze moved over us softly, the sun dots sparkled on the water, and the masts of the boats glistened in the slanting light.

It was wonderful to relax in contemplation of the scene, basking in the awareness of the change of climate, but life could not be all relaxation. Before we could be out there, with sails curved to the tradewind under those floating clouds, there were realities. Chores had to be done, like unpacking, shopping, fueling, taking on water, and trying to get the little glitches taken care of. I had come to realize that there is never a time in boat ownership when there are no little glitches to be solved.

Finally, forcing ourselves up from the breeze-sniffing, sunlight-absorbing lassitude of the breakfast table, we ambled back down the pier to Berth 17 on the south side, our home slip in what was to become our familiar neighborhood. Marina living has a form of back-fence friendliness, with the exchange of cocktail visits, swapping of sea stories, borrowing of tools and cups of sugar, and mutual support that added a pleasant dimension to the time we spent in port.

The link between all of us was Charlis (it took a while to be convinced that that was really how he spelled his name), the dock attendant. Over the years, we were to see him develop from a gangly youth to a mature adult, always with the same shy smile and semi-mumbled speech. He seemed the soul of relaxation, but he always managed to be right where a boat was entering or leaving a slip, and he got from one pier to the next with amazingly effortless speed.

He was there as we came back aboard, checking that our newly hooked-up electrical shore connection was OK and giving his own shy handshake of welcome. We had a few minutes of idle chatter, and he then moved on to help a boat down the pier clear out of a slip. The comings and goings of boats under the ministrations of Charlis were a continuing source of entertainment. Sometimes everything went smoothly, but there were also the occasional panic parties in which everyone from all the nearby slips ended up pushing and shoving, handling lines, and yelling instructions, as someone loused up a landing. I found that there was never anyone around when I made a smooth landing or departure, but the minute I got in some sort of fix, everybody in the marina seemed to be there to witness my shame.

Soon afterward, John Acland came to say hello. A slender, suave Englishman with reddish hair, glasses, and the usual soft, clipped accent, he was the marina manager, a genial host, and a source of support in whatever difficulties might arise. Since we had not discovered any serious ones yet, we merely had a pleasant chat, comparing notes and agreeing that it was great to be back.

It was an interesting "neighborhood." On the outboard side, a 42-foot sloop had a succession of visitors, mostly female, to the young man who was living aboard, evidently as a family boatkeeper. He was relaxed and friendly, and would give us raised eyebrows and a shrug when one of his visitors approached. Across the way, the charter schooner *White Squall,* a classic 80-foot two-master built of native New Zealand timber, which took people out on daysails, was operated by two New Zealand brothers-in-law, laid-back friendly types, who liked to share a beer over sea stories.

In the morning, a parade of tourists, hesitantly expectant, would wander down the pier two by two to board *White Squall,* and when she came back in late afternoon, they were a relaxed, jolly group who acted like lifelong friends.

The other slips across the pier were for transients, large auxiliaries and motor yachts that added an aura of glamour in their comings and goings. One of them was the lovely 62-foot motorsailer *Djinn,* owned by Harry and Catty Morgan as a descendant of the legendary J. P. Morgan *Corsairs,* with Tony and Jill Perry, a delightful British couple, aboard as professional crew and genial reunioners at happy hour.

The inboard slip was occupied by the 32-foot ketch *Carapace,* the winter retreat of Dr. Ben Spock and his new, much younger wife, Mary. We had met Ben and his first wife cruising in the Florida Keys over 20 years before, and it was good to catch up with him again. On that first encounter, we caught his name as "Sparks" for a while, and just knew him as an enthusiastic fellow sailor, but finally got him correctly identified. We had our three children with us, then in their early teens, and of course had the reaction of wondering how they shaped up under his observation. (Jane had followed Dr. Gesell's book, not Spock's, for advice on child-rearing, but we naturally did not mention that.)

Now he was approaching 80, but still vigorous and hearty, tall and well set-up. He had been an Olympic oarsman at Yale in 1924, with a cousin of mine as a crewmate, and he carried himself with a relaxed sense of physical power. He was deeply involved in operating and maintaining his boat, and fun and relaxing to be with on social visits. Mary was even more vigorous, in fact a "ball of fire," and always on the go. She was from Arkansas, with a voice that must have been trained in a local calling, as everything she said could be heard up and down the length of the pier. If Ben was off somewhere in the marina, her paging of him would drown out all other sound, and somehow she could manage to make a three-syllable sound out of calling the simple word "Ben." They made lively and fascinating neighbors.

There had been an amusing incident the previous year, when the marina was host to a U.S. Navy hydrofoil gunboat on a "state visit." She was a remarkable sight, with her foils folded up out of the water like some great nautical snowplow, and a forest of domes, bulbs, antennas and wiring overhead attesting to her electronic complexity. At first, everyone was excited by this exotic vessel, but it soon became apparent that there was a price to pay for the excitement. With all that electronic equipment, she had to keep everything charged and operating with the continuous, high, wailing drone of her generators, akin to a jet plane taxiing down the runway. Poor John Acland was besieged with complaints and politely asked the skipper if he couldn't switch to shore power.

"If you want us to black out the whole island in 30 seconds," was the answer, and we lived with the all-pervasive whine for two days. All this was right across from us and the Spocks, and speculation ran up and down the pier as to how one of the world's foremost pacifists would react to this ululating war machine. He, however, was deeply involved with repairing a leak under a lifeline stanchion and went his imperturbable way with no visible reaction, as the howling whine soared over his head.

But on this, our first day back, we merely had a cordial reunion and then went about the tasks of the day. Water was first, and Charlis helped us rig our hose from one of the spigots on the pier. There was always a problem with the way the water tasted after several months of non-use of the tanks. We never knew whether it was better to empty the tanks before layup, or to leave them full and then drain them when we started over again. Either way there was a mustiness until we had several tankfuls, and we used bottled water for coffee, tea, and drinking.

Then there were visits ashore to use the marina bathrooms. We had disconnected the miserable, howling, electricity-eating macerator-chlorinator when we left U.S. territorial waters. *Brunelle* could not be released from the builder's yard without one installed, under the ridiculous requirements governing pleasure boats, administered in New York, for example, by an office in the World Trade Center, where the entire sewage output of the complex went directly into the Hudson River. Offshore, however, we could be free of it, and its only drawback was that it took up space and had cost a pretty penny. In a confined marina, though, we always went ashore for the ritual morning visit.

Next came a rental car for doing errands, a Mini-Moke which seemed to fit right in with the BVI atmosphere, and I braced myself for left-hand driving. In addition to the wrong-side syndrome, it is a somewhat frightening hit-or-miss experience (miss, you hope) to mingle with the BVI drivers, many of whom have a sublime disregard of what most people consider proper driving habits. Not all of them: some are very polite and drive in snail-like timidity, but there is a noticeable minority whose modus operandi is to drive too fast, pass on curves, tailgate, play "boom-bass" radios at deafening volume, and live by the blare of a horn.

Driving the Mini-Moke, which is wide open to all outside influences, I felt nakedly defenseless, but I managed my errands without mishap, all properly on the left side, at the local shopping centers.

It is always a shock to come from marketing at home to food prices in the Caribbean, and to realize that the natives have to pay the same inflated costs as visitors. Shipping costs naturally boost the prices. (Liquor, however, is much cheaper.) There is no secret source of local bargains, though knowing the ropes can help in a few ways. Limes (imported) were three for a dollar at the supermarket, while juicier, but smaller, local ones could be bought down the street at a native stand for 50 cents a dozen. The Lagoon Plaza Drugstore had wonderful little sugar bananas at a reasonable price—a special treat, but this didn't last. The proprietor grew them on his own property up in the hills, but he eventually gave up the practice because so many of them were "liberated" off the trees.

At the other end of the scale was a snob appeal "gourmet" shop at the marina, run by a down-the-nose British couple who made you feel as though you were trespassing when they deigned to wait on you. Their prices were outrageous, calculated to stick yachtsmen who had not bothered to investigate further, and who might naturally feel that everything must be terribly good in such an atmosphere. Eventually we got to know the proprietors socially after being properly introduced at a party or two, and they became a bit more human. Their manner in the shop was a combination of calculated snob appeal and natural British reserve.

We only went to their shop in situations where it was inconvenient to go further afield in an "emergency" or sudden shortage, and our normal shopping was done at two supermarkets, The Circle and Rite-Way. Circle's big plus was that they would deliver, but Rite-Way was within walking distance if the order wasn't too bulky. With the Mini-Moke I could shop around, but a two-dollar taxi ride (as I said, American money is the local currency in the BVI) would bring you back from the Rite-Way if your order was too big to carry.

As a conscientious shopper (I do our shopping to save Jane the physical effort), I always tried to compare prices and look for bargains. I caused an amusing crisis when I found that Rite-Way was charging $2.40 for Fig Newtons (I am a Fig Newton freak), and a native general store, Franklin Market, an amazing catchall of everything from furniture, clothes, and plumbing supplies to Fig Newtons, had them for $1.62. I reported this to Peter Haycraft, the head of Rite-Way and one of the top local sailors, at a cocktail party, much to his consternation. He promised to investigate the situation immediately. (We went sailing soon after and did not have a chance to check results.)

Laying in the initial shopping of a season, with all those stock condiments, etc., is a major enterprise, but we finally got everything stowed. We had run the engine to shape up the refrigerator, and we were back in business.

Roland and Lisa, a German man and American woman on a Valiant 40, *Klee*, were in a nearby slip and came over for a reunion over cocktails. We had met them "down island" in Martinique the year before and now had one of those typical getting-back-together sessions cruising sailors have, immediately taking up where we had left off, as though it were yesterday, catching up with each others' cruising since then. Actually, it was a report by them of uncertain conditions in the lower Antilles that had influenced our decision to give up our Caribbean circumnavigation project and come back to the BVI.

Even though we were well-stocked, we were not quite ready to eat aboard yet, finding it easy to relax some more, and we still had the Mini-Moke, so we all drove over to the Mariners Inn at the Moorings Marina on the other side of the harbor, a pleasant open-air restaurant on the waterfront, looking out over their marina full of the company's charterboats. It is a relaxed, friendly place, with a maître d' and waitresses who greet you as though you lived there, with most of the tables occupied by charterers about to take off, or just finished, in Moorings boats. As usual, the local seafood was good, and we finished the evening with a return to one of our favorite cruising pastimes, listening to tapes (Glenn Miller and Ella Fitzgerald this time) in the cockpit over "chapeaux," our private fractured French for "nightcaps."

On checking through my logs, I find that we sometimes had, as on this night, what I always termed, in quotes, a "discussion," a euphemism for a normal marital disagreement. In retrospect, I can never remember what each one was about, but we always seemed to settle them (we're still married), and the log would usually then have a little * mark, which was my symbol for the way married couples normally make up.

There were more chores the next day, after a night of two rainsqualls, while we still had the Mini-Moke. I had a propane tank refilled and went to the CSY marina to try to find parts to repair the faulty latches and locker hasp, with semi-luck (one latch, no hasp).

5

UNDER SAIL

I TURNED IN the Mini-Moke, with the paperwork handled in an offhand manner by the wife of a Guyanan couple who ran the rental company. Never once looking at me, she unloaded a tirade to one of her employees about conditions at the emergency room of the local hospital. Quiet, skinny, and browbeaten, he seemed glad to slip out and drive me back to the boat, humming a little tune to himself under his breath.

In the afternoon, we backed out of the slip, no easy job in a confined space, with the wind usually blowing hard on the starboard quarter. No one was watching so I, of course, managed the tight turn to head out the basin without mishap. Auxiliaries are notoriously bad at backing up, and I never do it with confidence. I had been known to end up bumping around back at the slip's pilings when she backed up to windward to starboard too much, but not this time. We headed out of the marina and across the inner harbor to the fuel dock at The Moorings, the charter company marina across the way.

It is a very tight squeeze to get alongside the pumps at the confined inner end of the marina, and I still had "first-day-back" jitters, a chronic condition when you have been away for months. But the dock attendant for The Moorings took over when we got a line to him, and I let out a big sigh as we settled in. She took 25.7 gallons on 38 hours of operation, a $43 charge on the American Express card, and we weaved our way back over to Village Cay Marina without hitting anything.

We were now "in all respects ready for sea," as the old phrase in Navy orders has it, but it was late in the afternoon, so we had to wait until morning for our long-anticipated first sail of the season.

At cocktail time, a couple came wandering down the pier, stopping in front of each boat to point and make comments in the familiar pantomime of boat watchers in marinas the world over, and when they came to us, they gave a special cry of delight and came right down the finger pier to talk to us. They were a Canadian couple who were staying ashore here but who owned a CSY 37 in CSY's St. Vincent fleet, and they had to stop and chat when they saw another 37. The natural thing to do was to invite them aboard for a drink, and we had a pleasant time comparing notes. First of all they admired our blue color scheme, and they were interested in and impressed by the special features on *Brunelle* that were not on the standard charter-boats, like the extra ports, the gallows frame for the main boom, and the much larger, sturdier cockpit bimini.

After they left, we had our first dinner aboard, a simple one of lamb chops and peas, and our evening tapes were an interesting contrast, Boston Pops and Ray Noble, as we looked forward to sailing in the morning.

It rained heavily sometime around 0300, a noisy drumming on the deck overhead, along with splashing in the cockpit. The first drops woke me up and I got the hatch down before we got too wet. Water was blowing in through the cockpit porthole too, but we could leave the one on the port bulkhead open for a little bit of air. It is hard to sleep with the rain's intense assault right overhead, at least for me, but Jane could sleep through a tornado, I think. She burbled and whiffled happily, while I did the usual tossing and turning amid half-waking hallucinations.

It was still rainy in the morning, not promising for starting out, but this was to be the most relaxed kind of cruising as a lead-in to the season: no guests, no schedule, no designated destination, just sailing for the fun of it and getting back into the swing of things. By mid-morning, skies had opened up to large blue patches between friendlier looking clouds, the breeze had settled in nicely, and there was no reason to linger longer in Berth 17.

Once again I avoided disaster in maneuvering out, and, as we powered out the narrow channel between the jetties, feeling *Brunelle*'s first lift to the gentle harbor surge, Jane took the wheel and I busied myself at the mainsail cover. We had been giving the refrigerator its hour of engine and were nearing the end of it as increasing puffs of the trades skittered down on us from the lofty heights to the east of Road Harbour, and sunshine brightened through whiter, puffier clouds. As we neared the entrance buoy, I gave Jane a hand signal to put our bow into the wind while I hoisted the main, always a great feeling on the first sail of the season. When it was hand-hauled for

Brunelle in the Virgin Islands

three quarters of the way, then winched to full tension, I signaled her to head off to starboard to fill the sail, and I went back to the cockpit to trim it.

I might make a parenthetical comment here about hand signals. We had first seen them used by a Swedish couple who ran the ketch *Viking* on our first Caribbean charter cruise. Knowing that yelling in Swedish would tend to upset their charter guests, they developed a system of hand signals for all operations on deck, with smooth results, and we have used the same system ever since. It does not have to be complicated. Simple pointing for a course change, obvious stop and go signals for engine control, and forward and reverse motions. One signal I added was a slicing of the forefinger across the throat to signal for cutting the engine, and one nervous female guest was horrified at this when she saw it. She thought that Jane must have done something wrong and that I was going to cut her throat. It was an almost foolproof system, but I sometimes made a booboo when we would be entering a harbor, and one of the crew would be next to me up on the foredeck as we prepared to anchor. Forgetting for a moment that hand signals were in effect, I would see an interesting boat off to one side and point to it, and Jane would faithfully follow my false direction. Sometimes she knew what I was doing but would still pull the course change just to remind me to tend to business.

Now we settled on a close-hauled port tack, and then came the marvelously simple process of setting the roller-furling jib, a high-cut yankee. I cast off the furling line, and the sail snapped out nicely as I trimmed the sheet on the starboard self-tailing cockpit winch. *Brunelle* heeled to the new pressure, and she was under sail for the first time since May. It was time to kill the noise. I pulled the stop-control plunger up, heard the brief beep of the warning buzzer, pushed the plunger back down, turned off the ignition, and we relaxed into the blissful peace of a boat under sail. Both of us let out a heartfelt "Aaaaah!"

The peace is lack of engine noise, but not silence. There is the swish of water alongside, the hum of breeze through the shrouds, and the rhythmic chuckle of the bow wave. This was what we had been dreaming of on the hectic, sweaty bustle of the flight down, and the busy business of getting ready in Road Town. We were sailing.

I would wait and see whether to add the staysail to give us a double head-rig, as we would be beating eastward in Sir Francis Drake Channel. I held off a few moments to see how she was taking it.

Clearing out from the hills of Tortola, we felt the full sweep of Drake Channel, with the trades blowing unimpeded from the east at about 14–16 knots, ideal sailing for *Brunelle*. As ever, she handled the usual lively chop well. She is a dry boat, with a sea-kindly hull, and the only water that ever splashed aboard would be from an occasional maverick crest slopping in at a different angle from the wave pattern. Then she might throw a burst of spray, but this seldom would get as far aft as the cockpit. *Tanagra* had a center cockpit, and we were used to occasional dousings in it, so we appreciated the lessening of exposure in *Brunelle*'s aft one. This was not a heavy enough breeze to throw much spray, and I decided to add the staysail, boomed and self-trimming, to complete the rig. I balanced my way forward

Cooper Island

to the halyard at the mast, and she responded with a bit more drive right away. We settled back to enjoy Drake Channel on a long port tack to Salt Island, as Jane went back to her knitting and I relieved her at the wheel.

Drake Channel is one of the classic bodies of water in all the wide world of cruising. It received its name when Sir Francis Drake made a foray down it toward the Spanish stronghold at San Juan in the 16th century, after gathering his fleet in what is now known as Drake's Anchorage on the northwest side of Gorda Sound. The Spaniards were warned of his coming, probably by Indians, and the raid failed. If it had succeeded, the history of Puerto Rico, and many American cities, might have been very different.

The Channel is about 20 miles long. It starts in the west at the Narrows, which separate St. John in the USVI from Tortola by about a mile. From two to four miles wide on its eastward trend, it is bordered on the north by Tortola and Beef Island, and on the south by a string of lower islands: Peter, Dead Chest, Salt, Cooper, Ginger, Fallen Jerusalem and Virgin Gorda. At Virgin Gorda it tends northeastward and ends by meeting the Atlantic between the northwest tip of Virgin Gorda and a scattering of small islands of scrub and rock called The Dogs.

Road Harbour is its main port, eight miles west of the west end of Tortola (named, quite aptly, West End), and both sides of Drake Channel offer any number of anchorages. It is the heart of Virgin Island sailing in that wonderful combination of steady breeze in semiprotected water and a wide choice of harbors close at hand. The tradewind chop can be lively, especially where there are cuts into the Channel from the open Caribbean between the southern islands. The seas are short and fairly steep, but they do not have the open-ocean authority and majesty that is so close at hand in the Atlantic to the north and the Caribbean to the south, just beyond the lumpy barriers of islands.

A few other boats were out there on this improving day, dotted over the length of the Channel, but it was a bit early in the season for the great spread of sail that could be seen at the height of it in February–April. I sometimes amused myself by counting the boats in sight on one of those days and would occasionally get up into the 70s.

On a morning of warm-weather sailing, when all is right with the world, Jane and I have a little ritual game. As 1100 approaches, I don't make a thing out of looking at my watch or announcing the time. I just say "Well?" or sometimes merely raise my eyebrows when she happens to look at me, and without a word she goes below and picks a cold one out of the fridge. For many years it was usually a Saint Pauli Girl, but she had become harder to find lately, and the ritual now was for a sailor's standard "greenie," a Heineken. (Some people have started a rumor that the sunset green flash of the tropics is really just a reflection from sailors' greenies, but that can't be true any more, because we don't throw bottles over nowadays!)

We only do this ritual when everything is going just right, the breeze is fresh, and the sun is warm, and here it was the ultimate touch on our return to sailing Drake Channel.

We came up under Salt Island in a bit less than an hour, tacking onto starboard off the little panel of yellow sand at its western end. Salt is best known as the site of the wreck of the *Rhone*, a paddle-wheel steamer, in

1867. She had taken refuge in what was supposed to be the lee of Salt Island during a hurricane, only to be caught on a lee shore when the eye went over and reversed the wind 180 degrees. She was wrecked on the reefs off the point and is now the prime diving target of the area. Several dive boats were anchored there as we tacked over.

Salt Island gets its name from a modest spread of salt flats behind the beach. These are worked by members of the one family that lives on the island in several huts along the beach. They sell the salt commercially and also package it in small amounts as souvenirs for visitors. Miss Clementine, the "grande dame" of the clan, is a dignified meeter and greeter, who takes visitors on a mini-tour of the flats. It has been an interesting stop for our guests on occasion, but I always stay aboard, as the anchorage is an iffy one, a likely spot for dragging.

Now, as we headed off on starboard, I played my usual private game of trying to make Beef Island on one tack from here. Its impressive rounded hump, scene of the pirate massacre in colonial days, looms large to the northeast, and it always seems, as you tack over off Salt, that you can make it easily. But a combination of current and whimsical windshifts usually makes you fall below the original heading, ending up several hundred yards to leeward of Beef.

It is a notorious spot of confluence of conflicting currents and tricky windshifts around its perpendicular mass of cliffs streaked with gray stone. Daunting experience has taught me over the years not to cut close around it going in either direction. The tradewind waves rebound off its rocks in a bobble of reverse chop, and the wind shoots up its vertical face, leaving an area of comparative calm close to shore. Today everything was as expected—we sagged off to leeward under its southeastern point, so I headed out on port tack much farther than would seem necessary, avoiding the trap of sloppy seas and disappearing updrafts close inshore. We stayed in the full breeze by heading off for several hundred yards until we had a clear shot into Trellis Bay on starboard tack. Once again Beef Island had defeated me in my private game, but we finally mastered it.

Trellis Bay is one of our favorite anchorages. It is one of the few in the BVI with protection in all directions, and anchoring is easy in 8–10 foot depths and good holding ground in firm sand. Our 35-pound plow anchor always digs in well here. It is the home of The Last Resort, a unique restaurant-cum-nightclub on a tiny island in its center named Bellamy Cay (more about The Last Resort in pages to come). At this stage of the season, it was not yet open. Beef Island Airport is right next to Trellis on its western side, one of the few areas flat enough for an airstrip throughout the BVI. We often meet arriving guests and drop off departing ones right from the boat by anchoring close to the "town dock" for a 200-yard walk to the terminal.

We had no one to meet this time, as we had no guests scheduled until January, but I rowed the Avon ashore to reconfirm our return reservations at the ticket desk. Failure to do this can lead to all sorts of complications. Back aboard, I took a nap, one of my major in-port pleasures, and then we sighed happily over cocktail hour as the sun made its descent in the west, silhouetting the palm trees along the shore, standing blackly against the golden light in a pattern that has lured me into taking hundreds of photographs (of which one became the jacket photo of my book *Cruising the Easy Way*).

It is a lovely, peaceful time of day, with the breeze softening, the cumulus clouds over the Caribbean off to the east glowing salmon and gold in the dying light, and a fingernail of new moon appearing shyly over the sunset panoply. There is one feature of sunset time that we have grown used to, but that often sends newly arrived guests grabbing for sweaters or jackets. There is a quick temperature drop as the sun descends, perhaps from the mid-80s to mid-70s, which fools the newcomer into thinking the chill will last. Actually, the body quickly adjusts to the new, still-mild temperature, and the sensation is an ephemeral one.

This was a perfect coda to a day of celebrating being back, and we felt very much at home. It almost seemed an intrusion to bother with dinner, but, when the sunset brilliance faded through pastels to a luminous blue and the stars began to prick the darkened upper reaches of the sky, Jane did a quick job of warming up corned beef hash and canned peas. This has been our number-one standard cruising dinner since I spent the whole month of August, 1938 on my first self-operated cruise, living on this combination as the only dinner menu I knew how to cook, produced on a Sterno stove. Years later, I turned it out for Tony Bailey, a writer from the *New Yorker* magazine, who was aboard *Mar Claro* doing a piece on the start of the Bermuda Race. He described it in his article in "Talk of The Town" as "hash and peas splendid." Jane read it with some amazement, saying "YOU cooked?" It was probably the most amateurish cooking ever given an accolade in the *New Yorker*. Ever since then we refer to this dinner in one run together phrase, "hashandpeassplendid." It seemed splendid on this special night, as we capped it off with Mount Gay "chapeaux" and Benny Goodman tapes.

I had wisely assembled the bunk before dinner, and it was easy to slip below and slide into it.

The morning was cloudy, calm, and quite warm, not one for luring us into sailing, and we puttered, read, and napped all day. I stirred myself enough to clean the mildew off the underside of the bimini, not one of my favorite chores. The evening brought a change, as it began to rain hard, drumming on the deck in a tattoo for restless sleep, and—a rarity at this time of year—it kept up relentlessly through the next day. We put pots and buckets out on deck to catch rainwater for drinking, as we were still bothered by that mustiness in the tanks from summer layup, and it was a noisy, splashy day.

It also blew quite hard from the northeast, and Trellis Bay was a good place to be, as there is no room for waves to make up. By late afternoon the rain had stopped, but it was still very windy, and it was quite a different cocktail and dinner hour from the peaceful sunset of our first night. The wind whined through the shrouds and set up a vibration in the halyards that were tightly frapped away from the mast. If they had not been, there would have been a fearful racket of their clanging against the aluminum. Some boats in the anchorage were not as well tied-off, and their clatter added to the wind's symphony of sounds.

In all our times in the Caribbean, we had seldom seen rain hang on like this, perhaps only a couple of other times, but all our experience has been between mid-November and late May, when, unlike the summer, day-long steady rainfall is seldom encountered. We were just as glad we did not have guests aboard this time.

Two or three windblown-looking boats swept into the anchorage towards dusk and then put on one of those typical late afternoon entertainments in cruising harbors, making several unsuccessful stabs at coming to anchor. There is always much misdirected and misunderstood shouting, blowing away on the wind, and lots of ineffectual gesticulations. It is always nice to be snugly and smugly at anchor, feeling very superior, when this sort of show is acted out.

For a change of scene the following morning, even though it was still blowing in the 20s, we decided to head over to Virgin Gorda Yacht Harbour, seven miles to the east. It was a tough fight to wrestle the anchor up, as it had worked itself well down in Trellis Bay's firm sand. *Brunelle* came equipped with a power windlass, but it had popped its breaker the very first time I used it, and my attitude since then had been "The hell with it; just one more piece of machinery to worry over."

Usually I could manage the anchor by hand without too much trouble, but this time she was really in there, and it took some backing and filling under engine power to break it out.

Using the refrigerator hour, we powered through the messy bobble of wind vs. tide outside the harbor into the lee of Marina Cay to set reefed main and staysail, and we headed off for Virgin Gorda on port tack, with *Brunelle* once more proving her mettle by handling the conditions easily. She was dry slicing through the steep chop and was comfortable in making good progress. It was rewarding to see several other boats under power plunging up and down with minimum progress, and a boat or two with single headrigs wallowing and laboring under too much genoa, or else trying to make it under main alone.

In an hour and a half we were powering, via the L-shaped channel marked by tiny buoys, into Virgin Gorda Yacht Harbour's tight confines. We had checked by VHF on approach and had been directed to Berth 13 by Denise, the friendly voice of VGYH. At the slip we were greeted by the not-so-friendly dockmaster, for whom we had the private nickname of Grumpy Grampy. He always wore a fedora, the badge of authority among islanders, and he had a loud, gravelly voice ever at full volume. He had the heaviest island accent imaginable, completely incomprehensible to visitors, that BVI islanders use in talking to each other—but he used it all the time. There was almost total lack of understanding between him and the average American bareboat charterer trying to follow his instructions in making a landing. He would get angrier and angrier, yelling louder and louder, and it was something of a miracle that anyone was ever able to maneuver into a slip.

My favorite memory of him was the time that a couple came into the marina in a CSY 33 charter with the ridiculous name of *Itzabote*. They were obviously timid, inexperienced sailors, both hunched in life jackets, with the wife standing at the bow tentatively holding a dock line, and the husband peering anxiously around while gripping the wheel.

Grumpy Grampy stood on the pier, wanting to know if they had a reservation, and bellowed out, "What de name of you wessel?"

"*Itzabote*," came the meek reply from the woman.

"I KNOW it's a boat," Grumpy exploded. "What de name?"

Somehow it all straightened out without apoplexy as the result, but it always typified him to me. The only time I ever saw him smile was when I tipped him $10 for returning a credit card to me that I'd left in the marina office.

This day he was in his usual form, and I was in my usual form of having trouble backing. This was a slip with no finger pier, so the stern had to be in against the main pier for ease of getting ashore, compared to scrambling over the bow pulpit, and backing in was not going well. As he bellowed at me, we got skewed at an angle between the pilings, and there was all sorts of uproar before we finally settled in.

It was relief, then, to go to the marina office to check in and be greeted by Denise of the welcoming radio voice, a motherly well-rounded type with a wide, friendly face, and liquid, expressive eyes. I was always "Mr. Brunelle" to her, and she always made a great ceremony of returning my credit card after registering it as a reminder not to forget it this time.

VGYH was a place to stock up on supplies, as there were two markets and a bakery-cum-liquor store right at the marina, an operation of Rock Resorts, and convenient self-operated coin washing machines. While Jane patronized one of them, I did the shopping and walked down the beach to Fischer's Cove Hotel a few hundred yards away, to make a dinner reservation. It was native-run, with the restaurant right on the palm-fringed beach, an atmospheric spot for a casual dinner. We both had grouper, which was quite good. The walk back afterwards in the windy darkness had a feeling of loneliness and mystery, and getting back to *Brunelle* brought a reassuring sense of being home. Now that we had had a few days in her, we really had settled into that feeling of familiarity, of belonging. If it hadn't been blowing so hard, it would have felt even better, but sleep came easily in the security of the slip.

6

WHAT NEXT?

IT WAS STILL blowing hard in the morning, but we did not want to remain marina-bound, since we had done our shopping and laundry. One of the great assets of the BVI is the wide choice of harbors within easy reach. This is particularly so when the weather governs operations. In many cruising areas it is obligatory to head in one direction at a certain stage of a cruise, but here the choice is wide open, especially when you have made easting, as we had. Then, for over 90 percent of the time, the choice is downwind. Very often, as we did on this blustery morning, with low clouds shooting over us from the peaks of Virgin Gorda, we started out without having set a destination, simply letting nature take its course as the day progressed. I checked out with Denise, getting a cheery "Come back soon," and we at least had it easy leaving the slip, since we were stern-to. Grumpy Grampy was nowhere in sight, and we powered out the channel, rounding up outside to set reefed main and staysail. I mentally ticked off the choices we had.

Right across the way, of course, was Trellis Bay, and also Marina Cay. Trellis, as I have said, was one of our real favorites. Marina Cay, an anchorage tucked behind a fringing reef and the tiny cay itself, against the shore of hilly Great Camanoe Island, has a history. It was the subject of a memoir by Robb White called *Our Virgin Island*, about a young couple's adventures when they spent their honeymoon and built a house there back in the '30s. It was made into a movie, which marked the screen debut of Sidney Poitier as a friendly native who helped them, and it was followed by a sequel book, *Two on the Isle*, which, unhappily, revealed that the marriage ended in divorce. The strains of a long wartime separation had taken their toll.

In 1964, on our first VI cruise in the crewed charter yacht *Circe*, a 58-foot Herreshoff ketch out of St. Thomas, Marina Cay was the only place in the entire BVI where cruising yachtsmen could have dinner ashore. There was a dinghy pier alongside a tidy little beach, whose main feature was a large hammock strung between palm trees. The path led up the hill from here to the White's honeymoon cottage, still the main building and center of the resort, whose bedroom units were individual A-frames scattered atop the island's cliffs. Dinner at the cottage was family-style, with no menu choices, at a big community table. We had a pleasant time swapping sea stories with other diners, both guests and visiting sailors, and with the hosts, the Allan Bathams, a couple who exuded hospitality in the best British Empire style, making you feel like honored guests in their own home.

Among the guests a couple of young South African sailors who were crewing a charter yacht made quite a play for our daughter Martha, then aged 18. When we were ready to return to *Circe*, Martha asked if she could stay ashore longer, and the young men earnestly promised, "We'll take care of her, sir. We'll get her back aboard."

While we were "chapeauxing" back on *Circe*, at 2200 Marina Cay's generator whined to a thumping stop, and all the shore lights went out. "Hmmm," was my reaction. "How about Martha?"

We didn't wait up for her, but I kept an ear open and was happy to hear a dinghy alongside, with "Good nights" bandied softly about. In the morning, I casually asked Martha, "Where were you when the lights went out?"

She gave an embarrassed giggle and owned, "I was in that hammock fighting for my life!"

A couple of years later I ran into one of the South African Romeos, and he gulped "Oh oh," with a sheepish grin on his face when he recognized me.

And so Marina Cay had certain memories. It still retained its charm, and the hammock was there for years. The anchorage was one of the top spots on our BVI routine.

Northeast of VGYH, around the northwest tip of Virgin Gorda at rocky, spray-lashed Mountain Point, where the Atlantic meets Drake Channel, is Gorda Sound, also called North Sound, the cruising highlight of the BVI. Its two-by-three mile spread is bordered on the south and east by the heights of Virgin Gorda, and enclosed on the west and north by Mosquito and Prickly Pear Islands. It has a choice of several scenic anchorages and the resorts of Bitter End Yacht Club, Biras Creek, Drake's Anchorage, and Leverick Bay, plus the native village of Gun Creek. We always head there with guests aboard and never tire of its charms. In 1964, on the *Circe* cruise, there was nothing there but Gun Creek, and we were the only vessel in the whole place. With the cruising boom since then, its popularity has really blossomed, and there are always dozens of boats at anchor.

In the other direction, southwest of Virgin Gorda, is Cooper Island.

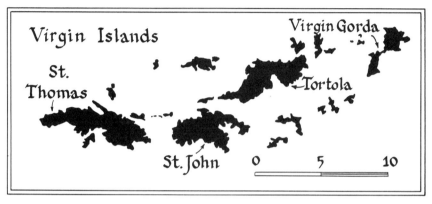

Map of the Virgin Islands

(Ginger has no harbor, except one tiny cove on its windward side where Ben Spock and Mary were once weathered in for almost two weeks.) Cooper has a few houses and a restaurant on its pleasant stretch of palm-shaded beach, a popular stop for lunch or dinner. The anchorage, technically on the leeward side, has drawbacks in not-too-solid holding ground and erratic breeze behavior. The trades blow over the top of its hill and then backwards down from the west against the beach, causing all sorts of confusion. Over the years, moorings have been added for use of restaurant guests, but none were there in this season.

Salt Island is only a day anchorage, as is Dead Man's Bay at the east end of Peter Island. It is just inside the steep, barren hunk of rock and scrub known as Dead Chest, which is supposedly the site of "Fifteen men on a dead man's chest. Yo, ho, ho, and a bottle of rum!" That makes a colorful story, but there is an island near Ponce on the south coast of Puerto Rico, called Muerte, about which the locals tell the same story, so you take your choice for a spot of local color—probably both apocryphal. Dead Man's Bay has a lovely, wide beach, but the anchorage is subject to surge, best only as a day stop. Sprat Bay, just west of Dead Man's, is the base for the fancy resort of Peter Island Yacht Club. It is snug and well-protected, but almost completely taken up with the resort's activities. We almost never visit PIYC, because jacket and tie are usually required in the dining room, a ridiculous idea in this part of the world, in our book.

Peter Island has Great Harbour, a wide bight midway along its north shore that is too deep for anchoring in all but one small area on its east side, but Little Harbour, just to the west of it, is one of the busiest BVI anchorages. This is partly because it is only about three miles on a direct reach across from Road Town, and most charterers, starting out in early afternoon after their briefing session, find it convenient just to duck in here.

On the other side of the Channel, Tortola offers East End, somewhat exposed on a shallow bay; Maya Cove, a landlocked base for charter yachts; Road Town, the metropolis; and a marina at Nanny Cay, three miles west of Road Town, a well set-up and very secure haven.

All these choices were there for us, and of course many more beyond Tortola at Norman Island and Jost Van Dyke, but we would not be heading that far.

My original thought was to head for North Sound, but as soon as we cleared Colison Point, the bold promontory just north of the marina, I changed my mind. The wind was in the northeast at a steady 22–24, with gusts over 30 swooping blackly across the water from the island's steep hills. There was a good sea running outside the point, and the nasty reef just offshore of it was a heaving, seething boil of breakers.

It would be a tough slog out to Mountain Point and around it, and my recently developed, relaxed approach to the cruising life convinced me that downwind was the way to go. It was a broad-off reach with a good heave of sea on our starboard quarter, and *Brunelle*'s round-bilged hull always set up quite a roll in these conditions. It was a fast, pendulum-like slide of about two hours to Peter Island's Little Harbour.

We have always had a special incentive for using Little Harbour. Not only is it picturesque in its circle of hills, palm-lined inner beach, and excellent protection from every direction but west, it also had a private mooring set out by Percy Chubb of the noted insurance family, for his fellow members (like me) in the Cruising Club of America. The Chubbs' winter home sat atop the hill that encloses Little Harbour on the north side, and Percy and his wife Corinne were always gracious hosts to CCA-ers who used the mooring.

A mooring is always a luxury for cruising sailors tired of hauling anchor, and it was a special, extra treat to have one in Little Harbour because of the peculiar wind behavior. There are hills of several hundred feet to the east, dropping steeply to the harbor, and this sets up an action I call "toilet bowling." Swooping down the slope and bouncing off the side hills, the wind goes into a circular motion that is completely unpredictable. This makes anchoring difficult, especially since the center of the harbor is quite deep, and the best procedure is usually to anchor fore-and-aft in the shallower water near shore. The first-day charterers who pop over from Road Town have a devil of a time getting settled in Little Harbour, and it is one of the major entertainments of cocktail time here to watch the goings on, especially while sitting serenely on the mooring (which is marked as a private one).

We had held off on lunch on the rolly run down Drake Channel, waiting till we were moored, and an experiment of using barbecue sauce in making shrimp salad was a noted failure. In another facet of my relaxed approach to cruising, I napped luxuriously all the gray afternoon, while Jane read Michener's *Chesapeake*. At cocktail time, a Cal 39, which had nosed tentatively in from Drake Channel, gave us the promised entertainment with over half an hour of backing, filling, setting anchor, and pulling it up again.

After dinner, as we listened to tapes of Ella (her straight singing, not scat), the sky finally began to clear, and there was the moon, now grown to a quarter, descending over St. John, with good old Orion, the one constellation besides the Dipper and Southern Cross that I can immediately identify, on his nightly journey overhead.

The clearing trend did not last overnight, and I used the cloudy, blowy morning to type a *Yachting* column. Dutifully, I ran the engine for the refrigerator hour, only to discover to my embarrassment at hour's end that I had never turned on the fridge switch. When I tried to restart the engine to make up for my mistake, there was a nasty, weak, whining sound and no response from the engine. Four-letter words!

What to do? At least Road Town was an easy sail across the way, so we hoisted the still-reefed main and got ready to sail off the mooring. I tried to pick an interval when the wind was steady in the east for a few minutes and dropped the mooring, but even before I could get back to the wheel, the wind did the "toilet bowl" trick around to the south, sending us directly across the narrow stretch of water toward the Chubbs' pier. It was a breath-holding moment until *Brunelle* responded, jibed over, and skinned by with a few feet to spare.

With staysail added we had a fast reach across the whitecapped gray of the Channel on the three miles to the CSY Marina. We had radioed ahead requesting a mechanic and someone to meet us at the end of the pier. The marina is directly under a 1000-foot peak on the east side of Road Harbour,

Brunelle

and is another spot with wildly erratic wind behavior, a tricky place to make a landing under sail. While you are approaching into an east wind, it might quit altogether or suddenly veer to a backwind, with instant changes in strength, and I was hoping to get in quickly and safely and get the sails down in a hurry.

As we luffed in against an easterly puff, no one was on the pier. Lunch hour—I forgot. Then a man, a charterer, not an employee, wandered over from one of the boats in a slip and stood hesitantly at the head of the pier. I threw him a long, light sheet as a heaving line and was ready to drop the sails, only to see that he was merely standing there with the line loose in his hand and a puzzled look on his face. Just then, a sideways gust caught us, and *Brunelle* veered wildly, parallel to the pier a few yards out. I let out an urgent yell, with gestures, for him to put the line on a bollard, and he did it just in time, awkwardly. *Brunelle* fetched up and lurched toward the pier, but Jane had a fender ready, and I quickly hopped ashore with another line, then scrambled back to the halyards. The sails came tumbling down, no damage had been done, and we breathed a large collective sigh.

But we still did not have an engine. Lunch hour continued, and no one came out to us for more than half an hour, while we grabbed a sandwich.

This was one of those "downer" times in cruising, a special experience for anyone like me who is not a natural mechanic. When you spend a lot of time with the moderately complicated arrangement of machinery and electrical gear and circuits that make up a cruising auxiliary, you are bound to have trouble from time to time. I have always lived with the knowledge that on any vessel more complicated than a rowboat there is always some item that is not functioning. It was certainly true on the Navy subchaser I commanded in World War II, but there I had a trained crew to handle the problems. It had always been true on my cruising boats, though I had kept *Mar Claro* as simple as possible for that reason, and, since the fuel gauge quit on *Brunelle*'s first day in commission, it was certainly true here, now and perpetually.

Except for the simplest problems, I have always been dependent on outside help in mechanical matters. It is a bit discouraging to realize how knowledgeable, skilled, and resourceful so many cruising sailors are in comparison to my ability to take things apart and lack of ability to put them together again. Often, I have received assistance from fellow sailors by acting helpless in a properly deferential manner, and it is also a fact that trained, professional mechanics are usually available in most popular cruising areas (except during lunch hour, as now). Still, it is always depressing, as of now, to have to worry about equipment failures that I can't handle.

The first attention we got was not from a mechanic, but from Eddie, a round-faced, smiling (gap-toothed) workman who had varnished *Brunelle*'s cabin sole the previous summer. He spied her at the end of the pier and came to see how his work had held up. He must have known that he had done a fine job, and I told him so. He was delighted to see how smooth and shiny everything still looked.

Speaking of brightwork, we have learned from very instructive experience not to have brightwork topsides in the Caribbean and other southern areas. *Brunelle* had none on deck, and boats that did have some were obviously a case of continuous, demanding maintenance.

We told Eddie we were very glad to see him, but where was the mechanic, and he gave a last admiring glance at his handiwork and said he would go find him. The mechanic, a serious, quiet man in greasy overalls, ambled down the pier in a while, listened to the feeble whine when the starter button was pushed, muttered "Bendix stuck," and quickly removed the offending item. He took it up to the shop and had it back in less than an hour, lubricated and working again. I listened in relief to the sound of the motor coughing to life, slipped him a twenty, and dropped off a short distance to one of CSY's moorings to spend the night.

Finally, the weather had returned to normal, and it was a clear, peaceful night, with the moon big enough to spread a path across the harbor, and the stars filled the sky, including Orion, of course. We now had just one day of sailing time before heading home for the traditional family Christmas, and we did not want to waste it, so we were at it early in the morning. The engine jumped to life in satisfying fashion for the refrigerator hour, and we were ready.

Early in the morning, an Esso tanker (no Exxon in this part of the world) had taken a mooring near us, dropped a stern anchor toward shore, and then run a hose over to CSY's tank. We maneuvered around her, feeling small but cleaner than she was, and made sail. The cruise ship *Vistafjord* was anchored just outside the entrance to the harbor, with her launches busily running passengers ashore, and we jogged around her, feeling even smaller as we gazed up at her impressive pale gray bulk, an unusual sight in these waters at the time, then headed out into a bright, clear, breezy tradewind day.

It was one for the pure enjoyment and relaxation of a good whole-sail breeze. We made a closehauled tack over to Cooper, taking a look at the new construction of the restaurant, then doused the jib and ran back west during cocktails and lunch. Cocktails consisted, as almost always, of Mount Gay on the rocks, which just seems to fit in well with the circumstances, and lunch was tuna salad, with tangerines and Fig Newtons of course, for dessert. We coasted along Salt and Dead Chest, poked right into Sprat Bay at Peter Island Yacht Club just for fun, then turned around and sailed over to circle *Vistafjord* again before reaching back to the CCA mooring at Little Harbour.

As so often happened, a charterboat was anchored quite close to the mooring, but they politely moved further away when they realized we wanted to pick it up. To thank them, I dinghied over, and ended up inviting them over for a drink. It was a Danish crew of three couples, with some brothers and sisters involved, and we could settle in over drinks by playing "Do you know?" about Danish yachting friends. They, of course, spoke English beautifully, a very cosmopolitan group, with one wife an Australian, and one of the couples, though Danish, living in Ibiza, where the husband was an architect. They had cruised many of the places we had, and we had a good time comparing notes. They were delighted that we had been to such Danish cruising ports as Marstal and Drejø and we had a "Skoal" over that.

They said it made them homesick, even though they were thoroughly enjoying themselves here.

For our last dinner aboard of this cruise we had, what else, "hashand-peassplendid" and watched the moon moving toward the west before early bedtime. Knowing we had all day to get to Village Cay, we had a lazy morning reading and swimming, and I took the dink and did some snorkeling on the tame but highly colorful coral heads close in along the north side of the harbor. There were teeming myriads of fish of every shade and hue, including one small barracuda. Corinne Chubb has always classified him as her pet, and he did the usual barracuda act of swimming warily nearby, with that glittering eye always focused on you.

Road Town is a guaranteed easy reach, which we did after lunch, not so sad that it was the last sail of this cruise, because we knew that we would be back again very soon. In this shakedown, we had set the stage for what we looked forward to as a new experience of cruising as the spirit moved, without having to get anywhere at any given time.

7

ENTERTAINING GUESTS

FROM NOW ON, we would no longer be cruising *à deux*. One of the chief pleasures in our cruising lifestyle has always been having family and friends aboard, as I have mentioned, and that would now be the routine for the rest of the winter. It is definitely a special pleasure, a means of much closer, concentrated contact and sharing than in activities on land, but it must be done correctly, with certain considerations and limitations. If things go wrong, they can really go wrong in the confines of a cruising boat. Later, we shall see the effects of this when I made the ill-advised move, against my better judgment, to take a "pier-head jump" passenger.

How we worked out our routines in handling guests aboard might provide helpful food for thought. Everyone has their own ideas, but ours did work out well, mostly, over long years of practice.

In entertaining family and friends, it is important to be selective, following certain rules, to insure compatibility. Of course you can't really be "selective" with family (unless there is an obvious, acknowledged incompatibility), but we fortunately have not had that problem. Our three offspring, who grew up with sailing as a major part of family life, all took to it enthusiastically. They enjoy cruising, and have been fine shipmates throughout. Now that grandchildren have entered the picture, a new dimension has been added, and again we have been lucky that it has "taken" with all of them, a wonderfully rewarding result. In the winter in question, though, they were still too young to be part of the picture.

Being selective with friends relates completely to the ability to live together harmoniously and rewardingly in a world measured by 37 (or whatever) feet. Some friends who are great fun at a dinner party or dance on shore are not necessarily good shipmates, and we made a mistake once that way—someone who wanted everything his way with no regard to the rest of the crew. Just as one example, he was a chain smoker who gave no heed to the effect this habit might have on others, both belowdecks and sitting to windward of them in the cockpit.

The formula for the compatibility of couples is heavily weighed in the way the women get along. Since Jane is very easy in this respect, things worked out well when she liked the other wife, and this was a basic of our invitations. Sometimes she was not too partial to the husband, but she let me worry about that.

It was not necessary for the guests to be experienced sailors, and many of them were not. We would advise ahead of time on things like luggage and shoes, and they were just happy to be there as long as there were no demands on them. We told them simply to sit tight and not worry, and if there was something they could do it would be explained in plain, non-nautical terms. Seasickness might be a problem, but fortunately not often, especially in the BVI, and medication like dramamine would help.

If they were experienced sailors, who sometimes had different ways of doing things from mine—not wrong, just different—I would explain mine and keep an eye on developments. For example, I have a thing about too-fancily coiled lines, such as halyard ends that are wrapped around and through-looped, looking very trim, but not handy for quick release when needed in a hurry. I prefer a coil that is attached to the cleat by a simple loop.

Of course it was usually a help to have an experienced sailor along to share the tasks, and most guests, even inexperienced ones, liked to take wheel tricks. Having someone help with the halyards, sail trim, anchor duty, dock lines, and fenders was a plus, even though Jane and I could manage very well on our own. Then I had my own little chores and routines, like checking lube oil, engine water, and fuel and water tanks, and I did not do maintenance chores when guests were aboard, since it was a short vacation for them.

Belowdecks, in the galley department, Jane was very much in charge, since she had her own routines for making things easy, knew where everything was, and seldom really needed help. However, the galley was well set-up for two people to have room to work, and Jane would use help that did not upset her routines, like buttering toast at breakfast or chopping celery for a lunch salad. It was always a plus to have help in cleaning up, and most guests were very willing to do the dishes once they had learned the easiest routine (and didn't waste too much water).

To make living aboard smoother in as painless a way as possible, I wrote up a list of "orders" in mock-serious Navy style, covering things like careful use of lights and water, returning items to their proper place, and operation of the stove and heads, with a few facetious comments about drinking and smoking, and a warning to obey the skipper's orders when boarding the dinghy. Impetuous, undirected moves in this department had caused some dunkings in the past.

Because turnover time was usually quite short and we were not always able to get laundry done, we normally asked guests to bring their own towels and bed linen. Laundry was easily done in Road Town or at other marinas, so it was just a question of time. We provided foul-weather gear unless someone really wanted to have their own, and it was seldom used anyway.

While in the BVI, meeting guests and sending them off was usually done very easily by anchoring in Trellis Bay off the airport, as I have mentioned. Given the on-time performance of the shuttle planes, I always took a crossword puzzle book with me to pass the waiting time. Crosswords were my favorite "time waster" on board. They fill in the periods of idle time very nicely, as idle time comes in rather short gaps when running a cruising boat. Jane is a constant reader, and I read occasionally, but crosswords are consumed like salted peanuts. I found that the average waiting time at Beef Island Airport was a "two-puzzler."

Guests often served a useful purpose as "couriers" of our mail. At the time, Martha was living near us in New Jersey, and she monitored our mail while we were on *Brunelle*. She and I had a joint checking account, and she paid our bills and deposited checks. Personal mail could be forwarded to us c/o Village Cay Marina or sent down via guests.

Speaking of bills, our usual financial arrangement with guests was to split food and liquor costs, but I would pay regular boat expenses like fuel, dockage, and professional assistance (mostly mechanics) as they would continue whether we had guests or not. In eating ashore, always a favorite pastime, we would usually have a "Captain's Dinner" and a "Crew's Dinner" and go Dutch the rest of the time. It would usually work out that we ate ashore two or three times a week as part of the adventure for guests, and as a relief for Jane from galley work. Since that original experience at Marina Cay in 1964, when it was the only place in the BVI to eat ashore, there was now a wide choice of spots in most of the harbors, and the other islands we visited had many interesting places and choice of cuisines: native, French, Chinese, Indonesian, and "International," which I guess is a fancy way of saying "just food."

Green Island, Antigua

As for entertainment built around the boat, much depended on guests' special interests and capabilities, but things did assume a fairly predictable pattern. Almost everyone wanted to swim in the delightful warm, clear water (that was also very salty), and we made allowances for that in our routine. Swimming from the boat meant a good ladder. My original purchase was a hopeless flexible rope affair that curved under the hull and was next to useless. This was replaced with a rigid wooden ladder that was stowed against the lifeline aft and rigged for use at the gate amidships to starboard. It was a very good ladder, but a nuisance to rig and unrig. We eventually ended up with a permanent folding metal ladder on the transom, a gift from a consortium of our guest "regulars" and an ideal solution. Night swimming was not advised.

The yawl *Iolaire* at The Baths, Virgin Gorda

For a post-swim shower, we had a "hot water bottle," a black plastic bag that would be placed on deck in the sun to warm the water and then hung from the rigging for gravitational use. Its hose was controlled by a simple snap clamp.

Along with the swimming, snorkeling was naturally a favorite. We had gear aboard in varying sizes, but some guests would bring their own to make sure of the fit. We had several favorite stops for snorkeling, and the usual cruising day would allow for a luncheon stop, very easy to do in the BVI and in almost all the areas we visited this winter. We did not have scuba gear, and none of our guests were scuba types. When our kids were much younger we sometimes sent them off for a day with scuba professionals, but snorkeling filled the bill for all hands now.

Many boats carry a sailboard or Sunfish for in-port fun. We did not, mainly because of space, but there were rental places where the younger in heart and build could indulge.

Beachcombing and exploring ashore have a fascination in spots like The Baths, Sandy Cay, the Caves, and many others in the BVI, as well as at Île Pinel in St. Martin, and Green Island and Five Islands in Antigua. Shell collectors especially love this, and we would make a point of allowing time. At the other end of the scale is shopping, and we would also allow time for this in the obvious areas. This would depend on the interest of women guests, and they varied considerably, from zero to fanatical. (Fortunately for me, Jane is near the zero end of the scale.) A quick classification of the shopping opportunities within our orbit that winter would be quaint for the BVI, routine in Antigua, and glitzy and bargain-oriented in duty-free St. Martin: Actually, I got a very good bargain in 7×50 binoculars in St. Martin, where optical and electronic bargains are real, and Jane could find her favorite perfume there at a good price.

When guests had special interests like bird watching or sightseeing and historic landmarks, we would try to cater to them. There is a form of sightseeing from the boat most of the time, but there are also on-land opportunities. Tortola, for example, has a magnificent scenic drive on its Ridge Road atop the island's backbone of steep hills, topped by Mt. Sage, which has a great nature walk through an unspoiled rain forest near its peak. We have had bird watchers aboard who, once they realized that pelicans, frigate birds, and boobies were completely routine, had a fine time ferreting out more exotic species in places like Peter Island, Virgin Gorda, and Anguilla.

All these are off-the-boat activities, but there is also the question of how much entertaining to organize on board. Naturally, the sheer joy of tradewind sailing is the main attraction, and we have never had anyone aboard who did not thrill to that.

Happy hour was always a pleasant interlude, which brings up the subject of alcohol. None of our regular guests had an alcohol "problem," and we would have been crazy to invite someone who did. There were many variations in the approach, and we had no hard and fast rules about the bar being closed, or someone helping themselves when they felt like it. Some people even liked to start the day with milk punches during a pre-breakfast swim, and since our friends were on a relatively short vacation, a little extra drinking would only be natural.

Since Jane and I were in for the long run, we had a fairly set routine of limiting our drinking to cocktails before lunch and dinner and the usual "chapeaux." Fortunately, we never had a problem with anyone's drinking, and it was a generally pleasant way of lubricating the atmosphere. Sometimes we had Scrabble games, but the main entertainments were reading, conversations, and listening to tapes while generally enjoying the atmosphere.

The question of fishing would occasionally come up. I am not a fisherman, except on a very casual basis, and I feel that fishing and a cruising sailboat are not exactly compatible due to the inevitable mess and odor. Another reason not to fish in northern Caribbean waters is the question of ciguatera. This is a disease that is very debilitating to humans, with nausea and cramps and a high fever. It starts in a fungus on coral reefs and spreads up the chain from small reef fish to the larger types that eat them and then are caught and eaten by people. Local commercial fishermen seem to know where to fish to avoid it, but the casual visitor cannot be sure.

So fishing was out, in my book, and I did not get many complaints, though our chain-smoking type did insist on bringing a surf-casting rod against my recommendation. This is a completely useless object in the BVI, and it was an awkward obstacle on the raised deck, the only place it could be stowed. He only used it once, from a calm-water beach at The Bitter End, and caught nothing. In a form of poetic justice, the airline lost it on the trip home.

The cruising life had its own built-in entertainment, and it was a major part of our pleasure to share it with congenial shipmates, invited because we knew that is what they would be.

8

A MONTH IN THE
BRITISH VIRGINS

AND THEY WERE.

For all of January we had good friends and family, and fortunately it was a typical month of BVI cruising under the best of conditions. There is a traditional feature in this part of the world called "Christmas Winds" which are supposed to start blowing over the holidays and continue well into January. Some years this is very true, and they can blow, staying in the 20s or higher for days on end. Some years they are a myth, never appearing, and in some years they can come in February or later, but are still called "Christmas Winds."

This January of 1981 was a mild one of normal trades in the mid-teens, and not much rain. We had a fine time in our new mode of aimless cruising. We did the usual rounds, enjoying the special charms of our favorite harbors with each group, not minding repeat visits, as each time we saw them through the eyes of new visitors.

It was a dramatic contrast to the Christmas junket home to an unusually cold New Jersey. We had the traditional family affair of 17 members finding places to sleep in every nook and cranny, and there was one amusing incident that related to *Brunelle*. While we were home, we had loaned her to John Yeoman, a young sailing and squash racquets friend who had helped us bring her partway down from Florida. As far as we knew, he was still aboard.

With the children just hustled off to bed with warnings about keeping Santa from his work, and the adults relaxing over a drink in front of the fire before tackling "Insert Tab A into Slot B" problems, there was a cry of "Ho, ho, ho" outside and a knock on the window. Surprise, surprise, there was John Yeoman in full Santa Claus costume, back home and having driven down from New York.

Naturally the kids were brought down for this "special occasion," and, depending on their age, were in various stages of astonishment. Martha's twins were the youngest and most goggle-eyed at age three, as John handed out presents from Santa's bag. Finally, they were herded back upstairs with admonishments about Santa having to finish his work, but twin Sam, ever the realist, looking at the blazing logs, planted himself in front of Santa and, lowering his head, said, "Let me see you go up the chimney."

It took some quick talking to resolve the crisis.

The trip home had been very much worth it, but now we were back after the usual sweaty fight through San Juan Airport, where Dorado Wings, a since deservedly defunct feeder line, screwed up the Beef Island connection with extra panache. We were traveling with the Tracys and Livengoods, best friends and frequent cruising companions. Somehow, the Tracys and Robinsons made Beef Island only an hour and a half late, but the Livengoods were two more hours behind.

Finally, though, there we were, relaxing in *Brunelle*'s cockpit at Village Cay Marina, where John Yeoman had left her in fine shape, on a night of soft breeze and bright stars, a long way from New Jersey and Santa Claus. Helen Tracy and Winkie Livengood were very best, lifelong friends of Jane's, and had formed, with Jane's sister Charlotte, an inseparable group known as the Beech-Broads, a title combining the two streets they lived on. We had all grown up together in Elizabeth, N.J., and the husbands, Ted Tracy and Hugh Livengood, had fit right into this special connection when they married into it. They were thoroughly familiar with Beech-Broad inside jokes and memories.

Ted, wiry, compact, and an ageless athlete, had looked and acted the same spry way ever since we had known him, an eager, enthusiastic participator. I had known Hugh, a neighbor two years ahead of me at our prep school, Pingry, since earliest childhood. He had had an unusual career, in that he had been a salesman for a steel company into mid-life, but had become increasingly involved in lay work in the Episcopal Church. In his mid-50s, he decided to enter the priesthood, went to seminary, and was ordained. He was extremely happy and rewarded in his new calling, but was far from "holier-than-thou." He was a wonderful shipmate, and we, of course, gave him responsibility for the weather, considering his special connections.

I mention all this background by way of explaining why we went against our usual rule of one couple at a time as guests. There was ample physical room on *Brunelle* for six if the mix was OK, and in this special case it certainly was. The same, of course, applied to family and one or two other special cases, as we shall see, but in general, one couple at a time is the best routine in entertaining guests.

The next guests would be one couple, my onetime Princeton roommate, Jack Haight, and Debbie. He was a history professor at Lehigh who seemed to have unlimited time off in winter breaks. Debbie, having spent every summer of her life at the little settlement of Desbarats, Ontario, for which she was phonetically named, on the North Channel of Lake Huron, was a more experienced sailor than Jack. They have a perpetual, enthusiastic interest in new experiences, always entering into new activities with gusto.

Following them, we were to have an unusual group, tabbed "The Trendy Trio," for two widows and a married man—Nancy Ruthrauff and Julia Gross, best friends for years and frequent cruising companions before and after widowhood, and their guide and escort, Joe Lord, a lifelong sailor whose wife was an invalid.

To complete our January of BVI cruising, our two daughters, Alice, unmarried and a yacht broker with John Alden Co., and Martha, divorced mother of three, who had a live-in sitter, were to be joined by Jim Simpson, widower and Helen Tracy's brother. He was another lifelong friend of both Jane's and mine, an eager, enthusiastic, come-lately-to-it sailor.

The sailing itineraries with each of these groups would more or less take in the same harbors, as they were our favorites. We wanted to show them off, and, as I have said, see them through fresh eyes each time.

Little Harbour would lead the list because of the private mooring, the swimming and snorkeling, and the pleasant visits to the Chubbs' house for cocktails. Percy, tall and slender, with a soft, precise way of speaking, was a gentleman of the old school. Most people would have yelled down from the hilltop house, "Hey, come on up," but Percy always walked down the hill, got in his rowboat, and rowed out to us with a gracious hello and a proper, formal invitation to join them.

It was always a treat for our guests (and for us) to see the house on its imposing site at the crest of a hilly point, with an all-encompassing view of Drake Channel from St. John and West End to Beef Island and Virgin Gorda. There was an enormous, airy living room, whose main features were a huge, classical breakfront (one couldn't help but wonder how it physically got there) and a wide terrace overlooking the harbor. Percy kept binoculars there, and he had his own version of our cocktail time entertainment, watching the misadventures and antics of boats trying to anchor. Most of our guests could pursue "Do-you-knows" with Chubbs and their house guests. Debbie Haight's father, "Dutch" Smith, for example, was an insurance executive and Percy of course knew him. Corinne, a sister of the Alsop newspaper columnists, was a brisk, commanding presence who made everyone feel very much at home.

In an attempt to repay some of their hospitality, we sometimes took the Chubbs and guests for a daysail. One time the guests were Katie and Waldo Howland of the well-known boatbuilding and yachting family from South Dartmouth, Mass. Waldo, head of the Concordia Company, and I had met casually through the boating world, and I knew he was noted for his championing of wooden boat construction and for his antipathy to fiberglass. He is an impish pixie of a man, short and stocky, with a twinkle in his eye and a laconic, New England way of talking, and I wondered how he would react to *Brunelle*'s fiberglass. I apologized to him in advance, and he just shrugged and said something like "Can't be helped." He seemed to be enjoying himself.

He steered for a while, and, since he was so short, I made another apology about the raised-deck cabin cutting visibility.

"Makes no difference," was his answer. "I'm so nearsighted I can't see the bow anyhow."

After a brisk sail out into Drake Channel, we reached back to The Bight at Norman Island and anchored for a swim and lunch. On the way back to Peter Island, we went through a brief but heavy squall, which *Brunelle* handled well under main and staysail after I rolled up the jib.

Everything I did all day was closely observed by Waldo, each time with questions about the gear and about what I was doing and why. When we got back to Little Harbour after an active day, the other daysailing guests were lavish with polite thanks, but Waldo's parting remark, in his best New England twang, was not a thank you. He just winked lightly and said, "Not goin' to worry about you any more."

We usually hit Virgin Gorda Yacht Harbour, which was normally a good, brisk three- to four-hour sail from Little Harbour, and we never failed to make The Bitter End. Marina Cay was another favorite, where we always got together with Fritz Seyfarth, the resident bard of the anchorage, who lived alone aboard his ancient Casey ketch *Tumbleweed*, anchored fore and aft (and sideways and backwards) just inside the reef at the entrance to Marina Cay. Fritz, an author who specializes in local color, as in his *Tales*

Exploring The Caves, Norman Island

of the Caribbean, and pirate lore, is a grizzled sea dog who has had all sorts of sailing adventures, and is a treasure chest of sea stories and the inside dope on local happenings—an extremely entertaining guest for cocktails and dinner.

Near Marina Cay is a special anchorage we like to think of as our own secret one. Evidently it is not touted to bareboat charterers in their briefing sessions, for we seldom see them there, but crewed boats sometimes stop in. It is called Monkey Point, a tiny bight at the south end of Guana Island, a northern satellite of Tortola. If there is no northerly surge, it is a perfect little lunchtime anchorage with some of the best snorkeling anywhere around, and we have made it one of our specialties. To get there from Trellis or Marina Cay requires threading a narrow channel between Great and Little Camanoe Islands and then heading over for a mile or so to Guana. The reefs along its rock-strewn beach teem with every variety of fish among the multi-hued coral heads, and snorkelers never fail to come back with ecstatic reports. Because of the marine life, the cove is also a favorite with pelicans, and on most days they put on a spectacular dive-bombing attack around the perimeter, turning in a moment from gracefully soaring fliers to folded-in missiles plummeting down to hit the water with a great splash. They are usually successful, and come up gulping down their prey with a great bobble of throat. We have never, however, seen a monkey here.

This is the only spot to anchor along the rugged north coast of Tortola, and it is a run of about seven miles in the open Atlantic around the northwest tip of Tortola and into Cane Garden Bay. This is a mountain-ringed half-moon of beautifully clear water, the most spectacular setting, and with the best beach in the BVI. An unpretentious native village lines the beach with a couple of bar-restaurants that are good local color, often with steel band music.

Five miles to the west is Jost Van Dyke, named for an old-time Dutch pirate, with anchorages at tiny, reef-girt White Bay, Great Harbour at the only "town," and Little Harbour, East End. In between Tortola and Jost is a gem of a little island called Sandy Cay, circled by white sand and with a nature walk, a very popular lunch stop. Exploring ashore here has always been a highlight for guests.

Swinging back east, Trellis Bay is where most of our weekly cruises end up, as we usually deliver people right to the airport from the boat. I have already described what a good anchorage it is, but its major attraction is The Last Resort, a low sprawl of buildings on tiny Bellamy Cay in the middle of the harbor, run by Jacquie and Tony Snell. The nightly buffet, with a wide choice of dishes, is among the best in the BVI for eating ashore. The star attraction is always roast beef and Yorkshire pudding (sort of like popovers to Americans). Boats make reservations by radio and the evening crowd piles ashore in a profusion of dinghies. Jacquie, ever smiling and friendly, supervises the kitchen with a loyal staff of local women, while raising a family of Jeremy and Jessica, who have grown from toddlers to teenagers in our years of coming here.

What really makes The Last Resort special, though, is the entertainment, a unique one-man show put on by Tony. He is a professional entertainer, with a London music hall background. (He was also a teenage RAF pilot in World War II.) Tall and handsome, he has a booming, completely distinctive laugh of very special timbre, and a strong, commanding voice, playing up the proper British accent. He operates at an electric organ on a small stage, with special noise-making machines that are amplified into a weird assortment of sound effects, and he also plays the guitar, ukulele and harmonica. His act is a mélange of satirical songs, mostly taking off the peccadilloes of bareboat sailors, with his own words to familiar tunes, interspersed with a patter of moderately risqué jokes, and then, every once in a while, a standard oldie thrown in straight. He punctuates his songs with his weird repertoire of sound effects and playback echoes, holding conversations with the playback, and he is a master at putting down anyone who dares to heckle him. His amplification is so powerful that we have actually heard him on a night of little breeze while we were anchored in Marina Cay over a mile away across the water.

There is all this and a donkey too. For years The Last Resort had Chocolate, an accurately named donkey, who had a special opening, decorated like a picture frame, through which she could poke her head into the club room from her grazing area in the yard, much to the amazement of first-time dinner guests. She would eat and drink anything offered (especially beer) and would sometimes take a nip at someone who didn't please her. Her sudden loud bray on occasion would always bring down the house.

As weekly regulars we got to be good friends with the Snells, had them aboard for lunch, and went to a party at a special place they had partway up Beef Island's imposing bulk at the remains of what had been the cattle-raising woman's plantation house in the 18th century. They had one room fitted out as a school for Jeremy and Jessica, with a resident tutor each year, and the usual schoolroom decorations of maps, pictures drawn by the kids, and alphabet letters strung around the top of the blackboard.

Jessica, then about eight, would often wander among the guests at the restaurant in the evening. On one of our visits she came up to Jane, seriously reproachful, and said, "I remember you. You went to sleep during my Daddy's act last week."

Trellis had another special attraction for me as the best harbor, because of low shoreline south and north, to see my favorite treat in the night sky, the Southern Cross and the Dipper and Polaris visible at the same time opposite each other. Even though this is about 18°N, the Cross rises high enough to clear the southern horizon by a few degrees for a couple of hours, and Polaris is always 18 degrees high in the northern sky, with the Dipper wheeling its nightly way around it. I did 90 percent of my celestial navigating in the Southern Hemisphere in the Navy and have always had a fond spot for the Cross. In January, it is only visible pre-dawn, and I always looked for it on my nightly visits to "God's great men's room" (the rail), usually at about 0400. By April it can be seen in late evening.

All these harbors were the stuff of our weekly routines, and there were other spots where we enjoyed eating ashore. At Virgin Gorda Yacht Harbour, the Olde Yard Inn, a restaurant up the hill from the marina, was run by friends of Debbie Haight's family, which made for a pleasant reunion. It was a friendly, intimate place with good food and an unusual added attraction, a library of fine editions, mostly of classics, protected from the climate by glass cases, and certainly an unexpected sight on a relatively primitive tropical island. The building had been a private home when the library was assembled by the owner, and the inn had maintained it as a distinctive feature.

At Bitter End Yacht Club, the highly organized dining room, feeding a great invasion of cruising sailors each night, was always a treat. We usually had lobster Bahamian, which was the native crawfish and a portion of mashed potato served in half a shell. The atmosphere was always one of sailors enjoying themselves on "shore leave," a lively celebration, and the evening would wind up in drinking coffee or tea on the terrace right at harbor's edge, with spiced rum added to the cup, and a lovely panorama of the lights of yachts in the anchorage. If it was the right week, the new moon was setting over the hills at the other end of North Sound.

Marina Cay still used the Robbs' original hilltop cottage as its family-style restaurant, though they added a waterfront bar and dining room for visiting sailors soon afterward. We liked Cooper Island for the easy informality of a beachfront lunch, and they did also serve dinner. Cane Garden and Jost Van Dyke featured native-style establishments in a very informal atmosphere, with especially good local seafood. At Nanny Cay there was Pegleg Landing, high on "stilts" right over the harbor, with a great view of Drake Channel and good food. Road Town had a wide choice of restaurants at the marinas and around town, and one special one, The Cloud Room (not to be confused with Sky World, a mountain-top restaurant on The Ridge Road).

The Cloud Room is on the top of Butu Mountain, 1200 feet above Road Town on the east, with a balcony off the dining room that hangs right out in space. The whole spread of Road Harbour, with its ring of lights, is down below, and on clear nights, the lights of St. Croix can be seen over 30 miles away. It is a spectacular spot to start things off with a drink. The place is run by the Paul Wattley family, Tortolans, and the only way to get there is to make a reservation for a pickup by Paul at a hotel or marina. Only a mountain goat or Paul's special bus can negotiate the rutted track up to it, and the ride always has a chorus of "oohs" and "aahs" and squeals from the passengers.

The food is well done, and the special feature of the dining room is a sliding roof. Paul is an accomplished architect, who designed the place himself, and this al fresco view of the stars, and the moon if it happens to be around, is a final touch to a unique place. It is always a hit with our crews, and we use it for special occasions, like our anniversary.

And so, our January weeks passed in these relaxing routines. The sailing was good every day, with special fun and loud cheers when the Flasher could be broken out. There had been very little rain, the swimming and snorkeling were fine, and the hours in *Brunelle*'s cockpit, reading, drinking, eating, listening to tapes, and just enjoying each other's company were well spent. It was a great cockpit for this kind of life—roomy, with comfortable seats and backrests for six or even eight, and a portable table attached to the binnacle for meals. We ate all our meals there, almost never forced below by the weather.

Another cockpit highlight would come during "happy hour" as evening fell. Writers over the centuries, mostly Englishmen used to the lingering twilights of northern latitudes, would often comment on the precipitate haste of tropical sundowns. True, they do not linger long, but there is a lovely period of half an hour or so when the descending sun first casts a golden glow on the ever-present towers of cumulus, followed moments later by a magic eight or ten minutes that we call "pink time" when the departed sun changes the cloud hue to a delicate pink, backed by the pure and equally delicate blue of the sky.

Pleasures like these were confirmation of what I have already said about the importance of the cockpit for successful cruising, a fact sometimes ignored in boats where a great fuss is made over the number of bunks crammed in (at the expense of cockpit space). It was a place to share memories of Beech-Broad days, and Jack Haight and I had college memories to laugh over, especially a (very informal) drinking group called the Friday Night Club. One of our most hilarious memories, which our wives never seemed to find quite so funny, involved a pool game when we were naked except for fedoras and neckties around our waists, in which I had pulled the great coup of sneaking a snowball in among the pool balls, with explosive reactions.

Music tapes were a source of nostalgia and enjoyment, and Debbie got so carried away by Glenn Miller's "In the Mood" that she managed to jitterbug around the few square feet of the cockpit.

New Year's Eve had been on our third night aboard with the Tracys and Livengoods. We were anchored at Marina Cay on a clear, calm night, and "chapeaux" in the cockpit had an extra dividend of a fireworks show from the island at about 2100. It was exciting and a special touch, but we were all in such a relaxed mood after our first sail of the cruise, highlighted by Winkie's glee on the helm in passing other boats, that none of us made it past 2200. Happy New Year!

There was one other notable incident in that first week. We went from Marina Cay over to Virgin Gorda Yacht Harbour and settled into a slip under Grumpy Grampy's direction. While I was putting *Brunelle* to bed, Hugh volunteered to rig the cord for the 110-volt shore power. The shore end went to an outlet at the head of the slip. With chores complete, I settled in the cockpit for a moment before going ashore to the marina shower room, and I began to smell a peculiar odor.

"Somebody's cooking something funny," was my first, wise-ass reaction, but I soon realized that it was closer to home than someone else's boat: Smoke was wisping out from the engine hatch in the cockpit sole, and I opened it. A good puff of acrid smoke came up from the area of the hot water tank, and I let out a surprised yelp. I made a quick decision that it must be something to do with shore power. I quickly unplugged the cord and then grabbed the engine room fire extinguisher and sprayed it on the source of smoke, a hose coming from the water heater.

The smoke subsided before any flames appeared, and everything seemed under control. I couldn't quite see how this had to do with shore power, but I went to investigate and found that we were somehow plugged in to 220 volts. The fitting on the pier had outlets for 110 and 220, neither one marked with identification, and the 220 one was so worn and splayed out that Hugh had managed to force the 110 plug end into it. What would have happened if we had all gone quickly ashore for showers was too horrendous to contemplate. As a result, the marina clearly marked all its outlets and replaced worn ones that could accept the wrong plug. Whew!

A narrow one, and Hugh was naturally distraught, but it really was not his fault. Fortunately, it had not gone on long enough to affect our wiring system. For some reason, the first effect had been in the wire reinforcing the water hose. It had taken the first shock, overheated, and started to burn the hose's rubber. An electrician checked everything out, the hose was replaced, the extinguisher mess cleaned up, the extinguisher recharged, and we were back in business.

The only other misadventure of the first crew's visit was that Ted Tracy, who was athletically coordinated enough to have made a spectacular split-second decision to leap into the dinghy when it broke loose one day in Little

Harbour, missed his step getting from the dinghy to the pier at Trellis Bay on the way to catching the plane. Ever the gentleman, he was properly dressed in a business suit, and it became a rather wet one for the flight.

The Haights' visit was a smooth one, with no untoward incidents, and, after they left, the next arrival was to be the "Trendy Trio." I went to the airport to meet them (45 minutes late; not bad for Dorado Wings), but all that got off the plane, however, was a "Distraught Duo."

Reeling across the tarmac with arms raised in triumph, Nancy and Julia made unsteady progress toward the Arrivals Gate, and I called down, "Where's Joe?"

"He couldn't come," was the wailing answer, followed by the triumphant shout, "But WE'RE HERE!"

It turned out that Joe had the flu and had had to cancel, but the ladies, bereft of guidance, braved the perils of the flight by themselves, somehow managing the daunting challenges both of Newark and San Juan Airports. Their travel procedure was a bit unusual. Despite the fact they were headed for the tropics and were in a heated limousine door-to-door, home to airport, they had dressed in full winter regalia leaving home, with winter underwear, woolen clothes, and overcoats, "in case the limo had a flat tire and we had to stand around outside." (I call this the really-looking-for-trouble mode of travel.) By the time they got to San Juan they were sweltering. They repaired to the ladies' room to get rid of some of their layers, but they were still warmly overdressed for arrival in the BVI.

Also, Nancy has an acute fear of heights and of flying, and she had only recently steeled herself to the rigors of air travel, using her own system to ward off the panic she always felt. She kept a modest flask of scotch in her purse, with frequent resort to nips from it for "courage." Julie, somewhat timid herself about air travel, and not wanting the problem of Nancy going too far with the scotch, brought a supply of Animal Crackers that she kept feeding Nancy. Joe normally smoothed everything out for them, and it was a major trauma to handle the adventure on their own. But they had made it!

There was one amusing incident when they were aboard. We went into Little Harbour to pick up the CCA mooring, and there was a small daysailer attached to it, with two men in bathing trunks sitting serenely in the cockpit. My usual procedure in this situation is to come close alongside and stare. The trespassers usually get the message and move, but not this time. Finally, in a flat Midlands accent, one of them said, "Got a problem, mate?"

I said that we had come in expressly to use that private mooring, and the response was, "You bloody Yanks think you can come down here and take over everything. We live here, and we don't like being pushed around. You think you own this mooring?"

"Look at the marking," I said, pointing to "CCA Mooring—Private." "Are you members of the Cruising Club?" I asked, my voice edged with sarcasm, and with this Jane, Julia, and Nancy slipped below, out of sight in the cabin.

"Cruising Club? What's that?" came the smarmy answer. "What do you have to do to belong?"

"You couldn't," I sneered in my smarmiest manner. "The dues are $40 a year."

"Oh, Bill. Be careful. Oh, Bill. Don't!" came pathetic wails from below, as they wigwagged negative gestures up at me, but I was in no mood to give in to the snotty so-and-sos.

We held position right there. I continued to glare at them, and they began to fidget, muttering to each other, and finally made motions about leaving. In a milder tone as they got ready to drop the line, I said, "It really is a private mooring."

This got no response other than a continual glare, but one of them pulled the outboard to life, the other dropped the line with a defiant splash, and they moved away. If looks could kill....

My crew began timidly to poke their heads up and then finally emerged. "Relax," I said. "They're gone."

Nancy had to fly home ahead of Julia, but she couldn't face flying alone. Fortunately, her son, John, was in Puerto Rico on business, and we were able to get him to come over, sail with us for a day, and escort his mother on the flight. Whether he had Animal Crackers, I don't know.

Daughter Martha replaced Nancy, arriving without incident, and we had a few good sails and one rather dégagée visit to Cane Garden, where we went to Stanley's Bar of steel band fame and Martha somehow got tangled with the Wofford College sailing team, who were there on a spring break charter cruise. The big sport at Stanley's was swinging in a rubber tire hanging from a tree.

Younger daughter Alice arrived and Julia flew home. Jim Simpson arrived via the most roundabout route over which anyone had ever joined us, all the way from Varna, Bulgaria, on the Black Sea, where he had been on business for Occidental Petroleum. Varna, Bulgaria, to Beef Island, BVI, sounds like one of those "you can't get there from here" setups, but Jim had made it, a little travel worn and jet-lagged.

We were in Trellis Bay, and he was immediately in the water, swimming laps around the boat in the beautiful stroke with which he had captained the Princeton swimming team in 1938. It always made me jealous to see his effortless form. Martha and Alice had had a day of windsurfing around Trellis Bay while we waited for Jim, and the athletic ambience was a bit different from the Distraught Duo.

We now had our crew together for pushing on into February and across Anegada Passage to the St. Martin area.

9

AGAINST THE WIND

EVEN UNDER MY new, relaxed approach to cruising the Caribbean, we were not ready to settle for the BVI for a whole winter. There was too much else to experience, and, with the younger generation as an inspiration and Jim's stalwart presence, it was an opportune time to move on to the east. We would miss the relaxed ease of BVI cruising, the friendly harbors, graceful scenery, gorgeously colored clear waters and steady breezes, but other areas had these too. We did now look on the BVI as our home base, and we would be back.

Incidentally, I had been offered a job by CSY to work on promotion and marketing of a maxi-yacht program they were planning to start, and my turndown was rapid. Who, me? Go back to work? No sir. Cruising was my life now.

We had one more day of local cruising before heading over Anegada Passage's 80 miles to St. Martin, and the morning routine was typical of most of the mornings of the past month. I did my small chores of checking battery water level and lube oil, taking the garbage to the community bin on shore, bringing the dinghy aboard, and doing the refrigerator hour on the engine, while the crew washed dishes. Then everyone got organized with head visits, sun cream application and locating reading material, knitting, or whatever. When everyone was ready, we got under way on the last of the refrigerator hour. Speaking of sun cream, we used No. 15 every day without fail.

On this day it was clear and breezy after some heavy early rain, and we got the anchor up, made sail outside the harbor, and headed for lunch at Cooper Island on a fast reach. Jim treated us to buffet lunch at the restaurant, where we sat at a big table with other sailors we knew. From there it was a vigorous beat in a freshening breeze to Virgin Gorda Yacht Harbour, where the new pier was in commission, with finger piers, so berthing was easy and Grumpy Grampy couldn't even scold us. Denise was as cordially welcoming as ever when I checked in at the marina office, congratulating her on the new facility.

We ate aboard and went in the evening to The Bath and Turtle, VGYH's "bistro" in the courtyard in the center of the shopping area, for some dancing to a native combo, part rock and roll, part calypso. It was crowded, noisy, and good, genial fun. Native young men invited Martha and Alice to dance, and everyone put on a good show.

The next day, February 2, saw the arrival of the "Christmas Winds," wouldn't you know, just when we were ready to head out to Anegada Passage. It was the strongest breeze of the new year, well up in the 20s, and was an example of why the Christmas Winds are often the butt of jokes. Any strong winter wind is blamed on them, right up to Mother's Day, or at least Easter.

We did final shopping, and I took a taxi, one of Speedy's, who seems to run everything on Virgin Gorda but the churches, to the airport. Customs and Immigration is there in a shack next to the daunting single runway, with lumpy hills at each end of its north-south alignment, directly crosswind to the prevailing trades. It is my least favorite airport in the few times we have had to use it. I much prefer coming to it by taxi than by plane.

After lunch, we took off and headed around Mountain Point with the option of continuing on to Anegada Passage or putting into Bitter End if the prospect was not encouraging. It was still blowing hard, and I began to make noises about spending the night at Bitter End to see what the morrow would bring.

Of my three children, Alice, the "baby," has always had the ability to control me by the mere lifting of an eyebrow. With her brother and sister, I argue, slam doors, and become dictatorial, but Alice just raises that brow and I collapse. This time, in addition to the left eye lift, she said dryly, referring back to one or two earlier experiences when we had been weatherbound, "Well, I guess I'll spend another cruise with my father sitting in a marina."

That's all it took. "OK, let's go," I said through clenched teeth as we approached Necker Island off North Sound, where the decision had to be made. Actually, the breeze seemed a bit less at the moment (I told myself). Hard on port tack under full sail, heeling well, we slid by Necker in smooth water at 1600 and stood out past the eastern end of Virgin Gorda into the open sea of Anegada Passage at 1800.

Anegada Passage is unique in the long arc of islands enclosing the Caribbean, first on the north and then on the east. It is the only inter-island

A Caribbean tradewind sea

passage from Cuba all the way to Grenada where you are out of sight of land for a while, and the 80 miles, normally of windward work, make the only section in that whole stretch that cannot be done in a day's sail. In addition, it is the meeting place of weather systems and currents from the Atlantic and the Caribbean that have no predictable pattern when they clash. The weather, therefore, is very changeable, and currents cannot be determined in advance.

I had heard tales of it for years and had read about its vagaries in many manuscripts submitted to *Yachting,* and we had done a round trip of it the previous winter. On both of those passages, we had started out in ideal conditions only to have a complete change of weather halfway across, with thundersqualls, heavy rain in short bursts, wind that played around in every direction, and from calm to gusts of 30 knots, plus incredibly lumpy, confused seas in no set pattern: Anegada Passage by the book.

Now we settled down to a good windward thrash in a chop of sea. She was doing well, but I thought a reef would be practical before dark, and it was a good decision. The breeze had a damp weight, and the sky had clouded over almost completely. It was not a time for dining off a table, and we had a finger-food supper of chicken Jane had cooked in port, plus celery, hard-boiled eggs, and apples. Alice and I were one watch (and never mentioned the decision to keep going), and Martha and Jim had the other: four on, four off.

It blew on harder after dark, and we doused the staysail. Twice, squalls hit hard enough for us to roll up the jib, easily done by running off momentarily to blanket it for quick furling. Eventually, we ended up under reefed main and staysail, all she would take without laboring. As we plugged on through a dark, cloudy, windy night with occasional squalls, and steadily increasing wind strength, that nighttime feeling that something menacing was up there ahead of us in the dark was a hard one to ignore in these conditions. A better rig for more power to push through the big, sloppy seas might have been a double-reefed main and the jib, but sail drill was not attractive, and she was handling it well enough. Squalls cleared away at dawn to reveal St. Martin as a dark lump well off on the windward horizon. Our heading was halfway between it and the purple cone of Saba far off to starboard.

It was slow progress over the confused lump of sea, and at 1030 I decided to motorsail at 1800 r.p.m. We plugged on port tack until 1300, when we could lay the island on starboard, and tacked over. After the damp chill of the night, the sun was hard and bright on the welter of sea, blasting against our wind-lashed, salt-streaked faces, and it was tough, hang-in-there going. Finally, at 1430, we were under the lee of the island and could douse sail and power directly in. It was 1600, exactly 24 hours from Necker Island, when we slid up to Bobby's Marina.

We had spent some time there on our way out and back last year, and we noticed right away that it had been expanded somewhat. Bobby Velasquez (the Bobby) was there to greet us like old friends, and he directed us to a berth on a mooring stern-to the southern side of the pier. Tall, husky, with olive skin, black hair and moustache, and always clad in immaculate, form-fitting dark coveralls, he has an accent all his own, a mix of British island singsong à la Bermuda or Barbados, and a South American lilt. He obviously had great plans for his marina, and the get-up-and-go to see them through. Over the years, each time we came back there were improvements, and the best of all was a breakwater that cut down the often horrendous surge. But that was in the future as we tied up. There was something of a surge, but not as bad as it could be. We had seen it when the dock was untenable.

It was a shock to go below after my almost uninterrupted 24 hours on deck to find the shambles that the rough going had created in the cabin, with books, clothes and miscellany in a jumble on the cabin sole. There was no real damage, however, and an hour of organizing by all hands had things back in shape. We had a couple of stiff drinks, raising our glasses to Anegada Passage and the conquering of it, a quickly thrown-together supper of canned stew and peas, followed by welcome oblivion in the sack at an early hour.

10

AN INTERESTING AREA, WITH COMPLICATIONS

ALTHOUGH WE'D HAD only had two short visits in this area the previous year, we felt at home and familiar as we settled in the next day, with the usual chores of getting organized in a new port. Immigration came first, with a visit to the police station. (Sint Maarten, the proper name for the Dutch half of the bi-national island, did not have Customs.) That bonus was balanced by some red tape about having to see the plane tickets of anyone who would by leaving by air, which meant a second visit. At the Great Bay Marina Commissary next door I bought a case of Mount Gay for $22.00, a bit more than my record price of $7.00 in Grenada in 1965, but still the best bargain so far in this era, and, another coup, I found a bottle of Crosse & Blackwell cocktail onions, an absolute must in a martini (Gibson), in my book.

Shopping was easy from Bobby's, with two markets within walking distance. Prices were in guilders, so it was hard to tell how high they were, but eventual familiarity confirmed that they were, as is usual throughout the Caribbean, in contrast with the good liquor prices. There were washing machines at Bobby's, so laundry was easy, and our demands are small in that department. T-shirts and polo shirts, all that we ever wear, do get sweaty in the climate, but we have a good supply, and, most of the time, I wear "jams" for pants. Martha, adept at such things, made several pairs for me. They are shorts with a built-in lining that double for regular wear and swimming, ideal on a boat, and they are more or less self-cleaning if you swim often enough. Jams

Philipsburg, St. Maarten

originated in Antigua, I believe, and Martha was able to duplicate them easily.

I also had some typing to do—*Yachting* columns and a book review—and I managed to make time for that. Jim and the girls were in a festive mood, which meant dinner at Antoine's, where you could easily imagine you were on New York's East Side, except for the clothing of the customers and the view of palms, beach, and boats outside. This was followed by a visit to a casino, where Jane and I were spectators and the others ruined their travel budgets.

And so we were settled into a new operating area for a while. Long a "No Man's Land" between the established centers of the Virgin Islands and Antigua, for years St. Martin had very little yachting, and it had only recently become popular in the cruising fraternity through the establishment of charter fleets and the beginnings of marinas, like Bobby's and Great Bay. It was still a shock to me to see these developments while remembering my first visit. That had been by air in 1958, when I had a few spare days to spend between other commitments. I had read about the "secret hideaway" of St. Martin and wanted to take a look. I came on an Air France DC–3 from San Juan, and I have two distinct memories of the

70

flight. One was that the very large island lady squeezed into the seat next to me had not bathed in quite some time, enveloping us in a pungent reminder of tropical living. The other was the slightly unsettling sight of the stewardess making several trips up the aisle with bottles of wine for the cockpit crew. Vive la France, n'est-ce pas?

At the time, the bay at Philipsburg was completely devoid of anything afloat, not even a rowboat, and the "main street" was a dusty village lane. There were two hotels on the whole island, Little Bay, where I stayed, then a small setup tucked away on a nice beach near town, and the Pasanggrahan, a guest house on the main street. The advances made in 23 years were startling, with large, Miami Beach–type hotels lining the south shore (Little Bay had quadrupled in size), a harbor full of anchored boats and the white bulk of cruise ships farther out, the two marinas, and the main street, now paved and lined with duty-free shops sporting credit card decals.

Holland and France have shared the island amicably for over 300 years, a unique arrangement in the Caribbean and probably in the world. The dividing line that gives Holland 16 square miles and France 21 was set, so the legend goes, by a Frenchman and a Dutchman starting out from a point on the west coast to walk around the island in opposite directions, with their meeting place on the east coast establishing the other end of the dividing line. There are no formalities in going from one side to the other. A small cairn of stones on the main road is the only reminder of international travel.

In 1958, the French side had been extremely primitive, a native fishing village with no hotels, restaurants, or tourist shops, and it was still catching up to the Dutch side in 1981. Several restaurants and boutiques had opened, with the ever-present decals in the windows, in the narrow-laned little town of Marigot, and each year it was becoming more and more sophisticated. The airport, barely big enough for a DC–3 in 1958, was now a major field for all big jets, with direct service to the U.S. and Europe, plus connections to all the Caribbean.

In our cruising here, we ended up establishing a routine, very much as in the BVI, with a much more limited choice of harbors. There are three main islands, the big one of St. Martin–Sint Maarten, Anguilla, and St. Barts, taking in three nationalities in their limited spread. On the south coast of Sint Maarten, Philipsburg and Simson Bay are it. Simson Lagoon is land-locked and a favorite hurricane hole, but at this time it could only be entered by arranging a special opening of the drawbridge on the main road to the airport—if you could find the bridge tender. It has been made more accessible in recent years both through that drawbridge and one at Marigot.

On the French side, Marigot is the main harbor, picturesque and well-protected in normal tradewind weather, but wide open to the rarity of a norther or a northerly surge. Grande Case and Anse Marcel are also good northside harbors with the same exposure, and Île Pinel, Green Island, and Oyster Pond are east-side spots, well-protected but sometimes difficult to negotiate if the easterly trades are too boisterous.

Anguilla, a British colony, has several harbors, with Road Bay on the north side the main one, and Rendezvous Bay the best on the south, but both have an open bearing. There is a tiny cove on Crocus Bay, and daytime beach stops at Sandy Cay, the Prickly Pear Cays, and Dog Island.

Gustavia is the main port of St. Barts, a French island with the unusual situation of a 95 percent white population. Its tiny inner harbor at Gustavia, whose name is a reminder that it was Swedish in the 19th century, once a smugglers' hideaway, is snug and chock-a-block with boats, and Baie Colombier at the northwest point has a lovely beach, but is surgy. There are a couple of day anchorages in settled weather on the windward side, and Île Fourche, between St. Martin and St. Barts, has a picturesque cove, looked over by five steep hills, that is a good lunch stop.

That's about it, and the distances are short, about 12 miles from Philipsburg to Marigot, six across to the western tip of Anguilla from there, and 14 miles from Philipsburg to Gustavia. Most of the sailing is fairly well protected except for the east side of St. Martin, when the trades have extra authority.

Our visitors for February after the "Trendy Trio Junior Grade" finished their time, were all friends and neighbors from home. Hazel and Dave Freeman were first. He and I had been clubmates at college, had been neighbors for years, and were long-time squash racqueters. They were not experienced sailors, but they loved new adventures and always fit in well, though Hazel was so polite and enthusiastic about everything that I used to tease her by begging her to complain about something. Between our house and the Freemans' on Oyster Bay Drive were the Lindemans, Connie and Neil, who were boatowners and lifelong sailors, much younger, and a great help in running the boat.

Coming between the Oyster Bay Drive groups, our very good friends, Gen and Al Gagnebin, had cruised with us many times in such diverse places as Buzzards Bay, the canals of France, and the Bahamas, and though they were older than we were, were always eager for adventure. Albert grew up in a French-speaking household, and he always reveled in acting as interpreter, so St. Martin was a good spot for him to use his skill. He had recently retired as Chairman of International Nickel Co., having worked his way up from a beginning job in the lab right out of college. A metallurgical engineer, he loved to tease me about my mechanical ineptitude as a "poet" and "artist," and I teased back that he was the only person I knew whose boat would suffer "stress corrosion cracking" in its rigging, which it did.

Our first day out in our new area after the night on the town at Antoine's and the casino, started with some unscheduled excitement, that, had we known, would be the forerunner of quite a bit more of the same. Bobby had been aboard for "chapeaux" after Jane and I returned from the casino the night before, and I had told him we needed to take on water. He said he would see to it in the morning. When morning came, still asleep I heard a banging around over my head, where the fuel and water intakes were located. I could hear Jim's and Bobby's voices, and the sound of a hose nozzle being inserted into an intake. Struggling into wakefulness, I realized that the inserting being done was the water hose into the diesel intake, and I sat up and yelled "No! No! Not in there; not in there!"

Jim had been on deck early, and Bobby, also up bright and early and remembering my request for water, had handed him the hose. By the time my yell stopped Jim, perhaps a quart of water had gone in, and we wondered what the result would be. The hose was switched to the proper intake and we topped off in the correct tank, with Jim shaking his head and apologizing profusely.

Meanwhile, there was all sorts of activity at the head of the pier with the arrival of *Enterprise,* a huge, white 120-foot Feadship motor yacht, run by the Amway Corp. as an employee recreation vessel. (If you sold more toilet brushes than anyone else, you got to ride on *Enterprise.*) She was the biggest thing that had ever happened to Bobby's, and there was all sorts of shoving, pushing, and yelling as she was sweated in alongside the end of the pier in what was not really a proper berth for her.

When things had settled down from that and we had gone through our morning routines, we were ready to set out for Anguilla, where we had a dinner engagement with friends of Jim's who had a house there. I wondered about the water in the diesel and ran the engine for 15 minutes as a test, without any problems, so we figured that there had not been enough water to cause trouble. We cast off, and immediately the engine died. We were just far enough out of the slip so that we could not get a line over and scramble back in. It was just a matter of seconds to break out the jib, one of the real benefits of roller-furling. It filled on a reach and took us on out into the harbor.

What the hell! The breeze was right, it was a beautiful day, and we did have a commitment, so we made full sail, swept by the white bulk of *Cunard Princess* anchored outside the bar, and headed out the harbor for the west end of the island on course for Anguilla. Martha and I spent over an hour at the fuel filter, clearing it of water, and working with the priming lever to bring more fuel through, with no results. So we kept sailing, and it was a beautiful day to be under way. St. Martin's mountains shone in the sun, and we left them rapidly behind on the reach to Anguillita, the little cay at Anguilla's western tip. We then beat our way up the north shore, where tropic birds, gracefully tern-like, with long, forked tails and red beaks, flew down from the colorfully streaked yellow cliffs and swooped around us with their piercing cries, their wings flashing in the sunlight, to anchor off the town pier in Road Bay at 1530 after a great sail (but still no engine).

We had a special friend in the little settlement called Sandy Ground at Road Bay—Emile Gumbs, the island government's Chief Minister, who lived just across the road from the pier in a house smothered in flowering shrubs. We had met him the previous year and had had several visits at his house. He and his attractive Canadian wife, Janice, had also been aboard for cocktails. I found them at home now and renewed our acquaintance over a cup of tea.

Emile is a tall, handsome man, deeply bronzed, with a full head of wavy iron-gray hair, whose family has lived on Anguilla, among the very few white residents, since the 18th century. An ardent sailor, very interested in the boats visiting Road Bay, he races one of the graceful, deep-keeled, native-style sailing dinghies that are hauled out in a row along Road Bay's beach, and for years was skipper of the family schooner, *Warspite*. She still sat at anchor in the harbor, her black hull gleaming in the slanting light, and a slightly lumpy sheer line testifying to her age—a lovely character vessel built in 1907. For years she had engaged in inter-island trade, and by this time was kept going as the supply vessel for Sombrero Light, the lonely manned lighthouse whose loom we had seen on our crossing, far out in Anegada Passage, as the first landfall of ships bound in from North America or Europe. Unfortunately, she was lost two years later when freak Hurricane Klaus roared through Road Bay from its wide-open bearing in the west.

When Emile heard my story about the engine, he offered to come have a look at it, but by the time we got aboard, Martha, the best mechanic in the family, and Jim had the engine purring away, and our troubles seemed to be solved.

Jim's friends had a house on the south shore of Anguilla, on a small bluff right over the beach, a lovely spot with a panoramic view of St. Martin's lumpy bulk across the six miles of Anguilla Channel, where the trade was ruffling the deep blue with a pattern of whitecaps. It was an interesting taxi ride over Anguilla's low hills, none more than 300 feet, past fields tended as farms and through the little mid-island settlement called The Valley, the nearest thing to a town on the island. Jim had known some of the people at the houseparty there, when he was in South America with W. R. Grace Co., so "old home week" sentiments prevailed.

Our pleasure was somewhat diminished the next morning when the engine would not start, but there was plenty of breeze under a cloud cover, and we had a fast sail back to Philipsburg. We made the six miles from Anguillita to Pointe Basse Terre at the western tip of St. Martin in 50 minutes, about as fast as a 29-foot waterline can sail, and we then had a good, hard thrash up the south coast, to pick up a mooring off Bobby's at 1530. There was all sorts of action there, as a barge was putting in extra pilings to make a more secure berth for *Enterprise*. Bobby was there, very much in command, strutting around at the end of the pier, and his shouted orders carried across the water.

As a farewell gesture on his last night, and to take our minds off engine troubles, Jim took us for dinner at Chesterfield's, a pleasant waterfront restaurant at Great Bay Marina, and the tournedos were good. Jane and I were happy to go back aboard, but, as a final fling, Jim took the girls dancing at a night club. Their arrival back aboard 0300 was not without a bit of noise, mainly giggles, and it sounded as though everyone had had a fine time. The girls later reported that Jim had gallantly danced the night away, taking turns, and they ended up telling him what a good sport he was. "And you're even older than Daddy!"

He headed for the airport in the morning, and the day was a messy one, taken up with the only way to solve the fuel problem: We were towed by Whaler into the pier, where a mechanic pumped out all the fuel, changed the filter, and bled the injectors. After three hours of this, the engine started happily, to restrained cheering, and purred away for over an hour, so our troubles seemed to be over. The mechanic somehow separated and saved 15 gallons of uncontaminated fuel to go back in the tank, and we then topped off with 45 gallons, which was interesting arithmetic for what the builders said was a 55-gallon tank. Anyway, we were back in business.

Fortunately it was a good day to be in port, as it was cloudy, with rain off and on all day. Meanwhile, the Freemans had arrived and checked in with us. They always like to combine a few days at a resort with cruising with us, and they were booked at the Summit Hotel for a few days. The Summit, logically enough, is high on a hill near a golf course, not on a beach, but overlooking the south shore with Saba's distinctive cone looming on the horizon. We taxied out there for dinner with them, and heavy spice seemed to be the hallmark of the cuisine.

The girls had stayed on *Brunelle*, and when we got back they were entertaining a husky, blond young man who was a steward on *Enterprise*. He had been a football player at the University of Delaware, and he was having trouble adapting to life as a servant, kowtowing to toilet brush salesmen from Amway. He was waiting it out with barely controlled impatience, standing by until the opportunity came for him to take tests for a job that was his life's ambition, an Atlantic City policeman. He said that it was a really great job, but we did not press him for details. Meanwhile, he did well by *Brunelle*'s beer supply.

It was great to have the daughters with us for a day or two more. Three years apart, they had never been very compatible as teenagers, as they were quite different personalities. We used to take them with us on Easter vacation cruises in the Caribbean that I was writing up for *Yachting,* and we worried about how they would get along in the confines of a cruising sailboat. One year, everything had gone surprisingly smoothly, and we congratulated them when we got home on how well they had done. They smiled a bit smugly and then fessed up. "We made a pact not to fight in front of you so we wouldn't spoil your trip...but you should have seen the fights we had when you couldn't hear us."

Now, as adults, they had adjusted well and admitted that they had really enjoyed being shipmates. We certainly enjoyed having them, as they had been both helpful and fun to be with.

With the Freemans aboard, Martha had to head back to her young brood, carrying mail (bills) and a manuscript with her for quicker postal action. Alice had another day, so we beat over to St. Barts in shifty winds and a lump of sea, since she had not been there before. The Freemans had been touted onto a restaurant, La Crémaillère, for dinner, and we were told during the afternoon that reservations were not necessary. At the door for dinner, we were greeted with supercilious reserve, and it took some talking to get us in. Then we sat for over an hour before anyone paid any attention to us. When we finally ate, it was quite good (lobster mayonnaise), but all this only reinforced my opinion of snooty French restaurants.

In a rarity, it was a peaceful, rainless night in our fore-and-aft anchorage in the tiny harbor. Boats were cheek-to-jowl only a few feet apart in the most intimate anchoring I have ever seen, and youngsters who lived aboard and were going to school there were on boats on each side of us, comparing their homework notes across our cockpit.

Not only is the harbor at Gustavia intimate; the town is as well. It was obviously built in the early 19th century, when Sweden owned it, and there is a European look to the houses and the narrow streets. Automobiles had never been thought of when these streets were laid out, and they are a real challenge for cars today—which does not stop the locals from barreling through at more than a safe rate of speed. It was, for many years, a smugglers' hideaway, with almost no tourism, and only recently have shops and restaurants been infused into the quaint old buildings, huddled together under overlooking hills. The social center, save for a bar or two, is the marine chandlery of Loulou Magras, located on a strategic corner just up the street from the waterfront. Loulou is an energetic, wiry Frenchman who is in complete touch with all marine happenings in the area, a personable meeter and greeter who makes everyone who enters his establishment feel immediately at home. His front door is a bulletin board for notices on everything marine, and personal ads for people selling boats or looking for crew berths. Given my opinion of how French yachtsmen anchor, and their harbor manners, I was amused to see an article from a Caribbean boating publication posted there, as it was a severe criticism of these habits. Loulou seems to know "where it's at."

Another facet of the intimate atmosphere of Gustavia is the noise, especially at the crack of dawn. As soon as the first light seeps over the hills, cocks crow, dogs bark, congregations sing hymns lustily in churches along the shore, church bells ring, and fishermen zoom off to their duties in 50-hp. outboards at full throttle. Sleep is a forgotten thing.

This was all right on that day, as we had to be under way fairly early to get Alice back to her plane at St. Martin, and we had a bit of shopping to do. I found that Mount Gay was $4 a case more than in St. Martin, a surprise in a port once famous for smugglers' bargain prices. Food shopping was handy in a waterfront market with more customers arriving by dinghy than by car. As in all the French islands, shopping for food was an adventure and a mystery in strange brands and packaging, in contrast to most of the rest of the Caribbean, where American brands are dominant.

Alice made her plane after a fast run dead downwind, and we were back to our usual two-couple arrangement with contemporaries.

II

"CHRISTMAS" IN FEBRUARY

ON AN EVENING of increasing clouds, we were comfortable on a mooring off Bobby's and ended up performing one of the rituals of cruising that is not a favorite of mine: cooking on the hibachi. *Brunelle* had one, and Jane was perpetually trying to coax me into using it, without success. But some of our guests seemed to think it was a privilege to be "allowed" to use it, and I never discouraged them. Dave Freeman was one of those, and he pitched in with gusto that night, with a fine production of lamb chops from the Gustavia market.

He had also contributed a guest's present to the boat of tapes that he had made specially, including Gilbert and Sullivan, Ella, and some classical music, and this night we had a classical concert.

As the clouds had foretold, the trades put on a February "Christmas Winds" performance, gusting over 30, and we had some fairly rugged sailing to get around to Marigot and Anguilla, including one day of waiting out really wild wind and rainsqualls in port at Marigot. At least Marigot had special charms for an enforced day of no sailing. First there was my custom of getting up and rowing ashore to a little beach that led up an alley to the boulangerie. The croissants here were something special, and so was my relationship with the baker's wife. I always spoke to her in French, and she always answered in English (and the croissants were marvelous).

Jane and Hazel had a fine visit to the native outdoor market along the harbor's edge, where they shopped with great deliberation, listening to the singsong sales pitches of the ladies who manned the stalls with shy little children peeking around their legs. They came back with limes, tomatoes, lettuce, tanya, cristofine, squash, bananas, and oranges. For lunch, we tried

Philipsburg harbor, looking at Saba

a new restaurant called La Vie en Rose next to the harbor. It was much more accommodating than the snooty place in St. Barts, with excellent salad based on the crispiest kind of lettuce. At siesta time, when the town was in a deathly hush, we walked around the narrow streets, with names like Rue C. de Gaulle and Rue de la Liberté where there was all sorts of construction, presaging the development that has gone on ever since.

I had to make a couple of phone calls to the States, not a wise idea from a French island, as they had never heard of credit cards, and collect calls take an hour and a half via Martinique, if you're lucky. The post office is the phone exchange, and I waited in line behind a woman tourist who was painstakingly buying one each of every stamp they had. When the clerk finally finished with all this, she took my calls, direct for cash, and they went through quickly enough, for $20.80.

We finally had a bit better weather for sailing to Anguilla, where Emile came aboard for dinner, but the sail back to Philipsburg was one for the books. It was blowing fresh from the east on a day of hard, bright sun, and, as we rounded Anguillita, we soon became aware that conditions were special. In open water it was not so noticeable that there were large swells, but Blowing Rock, a wicked, dark gray reef just above water off the southwest tip of Anguilla, was living up to its name in a fantastic show. Waves were breaking over it and sending great geysers of spray over a hundred feet into the air, while setting up an amazing boil and bubble of surf on the rock itself. As we approached Pointe Basse Terre on St. Martin, heavy surf could be seen breaking far up on the shore, sending great curtains of foam high above the normal waterline.

We radioed ahead to Bobby's for a berth, and the answer was that everyone had been evacuated from the pier because of surge. As we approached Great Bay at Philipsburg, we could see that the masts of boats at anchor were swinging like pendulums gone wild, and there was surf breaking over the six-foot bar halfway into the harbor, with young surfers riding the curling waves in what was usually an anchoring area.

In all this wild commotion, the best spot seemed to be close inshore, just south of Great Bay Marina. Fortunately, there was room enough for us to anchor. We were heaving and rolling, but nothing like the fantastic antics of the boats farther out in the middle of the bay. I have been in some surgy harbors over the years, but nothing to compare with this unbelievable scene. Where we were was just close enough under Pointe Blanche at the southwest tip of the island, with its long cruise ship pier extending out into the harbor, that the worst of the surge was diverted a bit offshore from us. The strong winds of the last few days had evidently set up the big swells, and Philipsburg is very vulnerable to any surge coming in from south of east.

It was an acrobatic feat to get ashore from the dinghy at Great Bay Marina, but I somehow managed it without a dunking and did some business in town. We had planned to eat ashore at La Grenouille, one of the fancier French restaurants, but the thought of getting four of us safely out of the dinghy was a daunting one, and we settled for ham and succotash on board, and early bed. I was pleasantly surprised at how *Brunelle* rode during the night, with williwaws sweeping down on us over the eastern hills in our position right under them. At least there was no rain, and the morning revealed a bright, breezy day with a somewhat modified surge; and the surfers were no longer riding the waves on the central bar.

The Freemans were due to leave later in the day and wanted to explore (translate "shop") on shore in the morning. I managed to get them safely out of the dinghy, and was back on board, typing a column, when I heard a crash and a thump up forward. Hopping on deck, I found a sloop bouncing up and down at our bow in what was still a considerable surge, with its anchor rode draped across ours.

It was the ultimate in the type of French cruising boat that we have now and then encountered in the Caribbean, and one whose owner had obviously not read the article posted on Loulou's door in Gustavia. Its stained metal hull was a strange off-color purple, and its cabin was a bilious green. Its deck seemed to be covered in gravel, and odd parts of bicycles were strewn about, along with buckets, pieces of rope, and unidentified piles of junk. The lone person aboard was a scruffily bearded, long-haired man clad only in a dirty bikini bottom. He and a mangy looking cat were glaring up at me, and he was at his steering station making motions about turning on the engine.

Since my anchor line was caught under his keel, near the rudder, as he had dragged over it, I could see the imminent cutting of the line and loss of my 35-lb. plow if he put his engine in gear. I yelled a very definite "No, No, No!" at him. Fortunately, he paused, and the cat let out a nasty yowl. The boat was bumping up under our bow, which was having a deleterious effect on his rickety-looking lifelines. I could sympathize with his desire to get out of there, but not at the expense of my anchor.

We had a conversation of sorts in fractured Frenglish, with my part mainly consisting of "No engine. No engine!" (Or maybe it was "Pas de engine!") He kept looking over the side and shrugging. I must admit that I had not reached any conclusion on how to solve the mess, when he picked up a weighted diving belt from the junk piles on his deck and pointed to my rode.

Meanwhile, Jane, who does not like to see me involved in altercations, as with the snotty Limeys on the CCA mooring at Little Harbour, was staying judiciously away in our cockpit.

He gestured that he would hang the belt on my rode, with a line on it, while I slacked off on our rode. The weight of the belt, and the lack of tension for a few moments, would lower our line, and he could float free. Wonder of wonders, it worked. I took the control line of the weight on board and slacked off our anchor while letting the weight slide down it. He had already brought his anchor up, so he floated free and drifted off astern, with the cat still screeching at me. He circled around astern of us until I dinghied over to him with the weight, which he grabbed from me without a word or gesture as I handed it up to him. He then moved off to anchor, dropping the hook some distance off our stern, and was soon dragging merrily off to leeward. Fortunately, I never saw him again.

The Freemans got away safely, and we then moved closer to Bobby's, where we were to meet the Gagnebins. The surge was slowly moderating, though still noticeable, and it was a major feat to get the Gagnebins aboard when they arrived in early evening. We met them at the pier at Bobby's, which was still devoid of boats, and came to the mutual decision to eat ashore at the beachfront restaurant next to the marina before braving the dink. Finally, however, we had to face up to the challenge. Both the

Gagnebins were in their 70s and of solid build, not what you would call agile athletes. Also, they had been doing considerable other travel, staying in hotels, and they apologized that their luggage was heavy and not nautically oriented.

I had brought the swimming ladder with us to help in the transfer down to the dink, as there was nothing like a ladder or dinghy float in the marina. The good old Avon, her black rubber shining in the lights from the pier, was swooping around in the surge, sliding under the pier and charging back out to bang up hard at the end of her painter; but, by standing in it and keeping a firm grip on the pier, I could stop the gyrations and hold her steady.

A rubber boat is not the handiest craft to get into in the calmest circumstances, and we have had guests go ass-over-teakettle into the water in the process, but one by one, Gen, Jane and Al came carefully down the ladder, and, despite how heavily laden we were, all was finally secure. We held our breath on the short row to the mooring, and then once more went through the steadying act while they went up the ladder and into the cockpit. The ladder was that sturdy, straight wooden one that we lashed at the midships gate of the lifeline, and I was glad that I had replaced our original rope ladder, a very poor, flexible hazard, with this stalwart one. We could not have managed the transfer with the old one. This was before the days of the permanently installed fold-up ladder on the transom, which we wouldn't have taken to the pier in any case.

My anticipation that cruising in this area would be in a routine similar to that in the BVI was a bit optimistic. We did visit virtually the same set of harbors with each set of guests, but this Christmas-Windy February made each "routine" cruise quite an adventure, even if we had not gotten water in the diesel or tangled with the French "seaman" and his cat.

With the Gagnebins aboard, the first of these adventures was to take on water. We were just about out, and we therefore had to manage coming into Bobby's pier to fill up, as there was no alternate place in the area. Once alongside, it was very obvious that the surge was still with us. Not too bad at anchor or on a mooring, it showed its real power when you were at something as solid and stable as a pier. We were to pick up a berth mooring and then drop back stern-to the pier, but the mooring we were directed to was tangled with another one, and it was a tricky fight to get it aboard. Somehow we managed, and took on water as quickly as we could (in the right intake this time!) while *Brunelle* slammed and banged back and forth between the mooring and the dock lines. Then we got the hell out of there with a great sigh of relief.

Jane and Bill Robinson

Fortunately, Al Gagnebin revels in strong sailing breezes, and Gen allows him his enthusiasm, as we had those conditions for the entire week. At Marigot we had a good dinner at another new restaurant on the waterfront called Le Nadaillac, where my noisettes of veal were fine and so was Jane's red snapper. At Anguilla, we tried Rendezvous Bay for a luncheon swim on a beautiful but windy day, and then had a real, rail-down beat into Road Bay. My visit to Immigration there cost me $4 for two tickets to the Policemen's Ball and a $25 bill from the policeman's wife for doing laundry.

It was a gorgeous, clear night of almost full moon making a path across the water, but the morning was squally and stormy, not a day for sailing. We relaxed aboard until a teatime visit with the Gumbs. I use days like this for minor chores, and I fixed the port running light and did Nev-R-Dul (a process I find Ver-i-Dul, but necessary) on the stanchions and bimini supports.

A visit to the Gumbs is always a treat. Their house was built by Emile's grandfather in the 19th century, and it is surrounded by flower beds and shrubs. They live on the second floor and have an apartment down below for family or rental visits. Their living room has lovely old period furniture, with cheerful decorations, and it is a gracious, old-time ceremony to have tea there.

Dinner back aboard was a good one of steak and cristofine, a squashlike vegetable that Jane has learned to cook with ginger. It is spiny, and she handles it while preparing it by greasing her hands with margarine to thwart the prickles—advice handed out by the motherly ladies who sell the stuff in their native market stalls.

Our sail back to the French side of St. Martin was under reefed main and staysail in 30 knots of wind and heavy seas, and *Brunelle* did herself proud, making good, and dry, progress into Potence Bay on the east side of Marigot Harbour on one tack from Anguillita. We then tacked around the point into Grande Case, where we anchored close into its big, beautiful beach in ten feet of water.

We had arranged to meet friends of the Gagnebins, who lived on St. Martin, for dinner at a restaurant here, one of the many strung along the beach, called Chez Cristofine. My lobster was good but Jane's was not, and the special entertainment was in watching rats scurry back and forth along a beam high on the wall. Under a full moon, *Brunelle* spent the night swinging wildly around her anchor to williwaws and erratic gusts that shot over the low saddle between the hills inshore of us.

Al's strong breezes continued. To go on to St. Barts we had another windward slug under reefed main and staysail through big, tradewind seas in a lumpy, erratic pattern, and *Brunelle* again showed her ability to tough it out through these conditions. We squeezed our way into Gustavia's cozy confines, had a visit at cocktails from friends of friends who recognized *Brunelle*, and decided to have dinner aboard under the full moon, which was gorgeous when there were not quick little rain clouds flitting by.

On the way back to Philipsburg, the breeze finally moderated for the Gagnebins' last day, and we broke the crossing with a lunch stop at Baie Colombier under the hill topped by the impressive winter home of David Rockefeller. While the Gagnebins explored the beach, I used swim time for one of those little chores that crop up after time spent in crowded commercial harbors like Philipsburg and Gustavia—cleaning off scum that had collected along the waterline.

Although the breeze had moderated for the run to Philipsburg, the swells were still impressive, and *Brunelle* did her thing of proving that she was not perfect in every way by rolling heavily as we surged along (but any monohull would have). Again we had trouble with a berth-mooring at

Bobby's that pulled loose when we picked it up, but we finally got settled just in time for a major celebration, expansively hosted by Bobby, christening *Enterprise*'s new section of pier. Incredibly loud music blared from her loudspeakers, and Bobby, still in overalls, continually made the rounds dispensing champagne to all hands, including everyone from the berthed boats, who were screaming to be heard above the music. *Enterprise*'s officers, in their crisp, spotless whites, looking like admirals of the fleet, mixed in with the more scruffily dressed yachtsmen, and it was a gala affair.

The Gagnebins' "crew's dinner" was a pleasant contrast in the peaceful surroundings of La Grenouille on the second floor of a beachfront building, with a view through palm trees to what was left of the surge fanning across the pale sand. Later, the moon slanted its path toward us to complement the scene, while I enjoyed quail and Jane, trying again, had better lobster than at Grande Case.

It was a quick crew change, as the Gagnebins left in the morning and the Lindemans arrived in mid-afternoon, with just enough time in between for food and liquor shopping.

The surge was still banging us back and forth enough at the pier to make us pull out to a mooring, where we rode better until, with the wind now totally calm, we tended into the beach at a different angle from the usual one and bounced once on the bottom at 0400, a sure way to interrupt sleep. I shortened the mooring pendant, and we bounced no more.

It was time to face Anegada Passage again, as we were due back in the BVI for several commitments. Now the usual prospect was for a downwind slide, making it less daunting than the eastbound crossing, but the wind had quit completely. Instead of powering across, we decided to give the Lindemans a taste of the Gallic life with a last visit to Marigot. Properly dressed in what we were told were the required long pants, we tried still another of the new French restaurants, La Calanque, where the coquilles St. Jacques were excellent.

In the morning there were, of course, the obligatory croissants, and now that we were ready to go, the wind had come in fresh from the northwest, swinging us around so that our stern was only about 20 feet off the reef that lined the boulangerie beach. We moved farther out as soon as I came back with the croissants, while a local fisherman near us in a dinghy tut-tutted at us and pointed to the reef. We wanted to make an afternoon departure, and did not relish bouncing around all day in the good sea running in the now-exposed anchorage, so we tacked across Anguilla Passage to Rendezvous Bay for lunch and a swim, and I built a little reserve for the long night ahead by taking a nap.

At 1600, under full sail, we started out in a still freshening nor'wester, finishing off the "routines" of the St. Martin area with still another non-routine situation.

12

NORTHERS, WHALES, AND OTHER AMUSEMENTS

THERE IT WAS, the only norther of the winter to reach this far into the Caribbean, and we had it for what should have been a tradewind run back to the BVI. At least the sky was clear, and the waning moon shone brightly when it appeared. What it shone on was a wildly unpatterned lump of sea kicked up by the fresh norther. In the lee of Anguilla in smooth sea we had been under full sail, but once past Anguilla (and a subdued Blowing Rock), with our bow pointed at the clear gold of the sunset, the wind had more heft, a bit over 20, and the seas built up in their helter-skelter fashion.

We ended up under reefed main and staysail, as it would have been a real slam-bang bouncer to force her through the seas with more sail power. We were not racing (by a long shot), and we jogged along on 285°M with plenty of motion, but not the urgent crash and smash there could have been. We split four-hour watches with the Lindemans, and the wind gradually faired us from a close reach to a broad one. In contrast to the closed-in feeling of the black, clouded eastbound night, there was a sense of the space and glittery distance on the open sea as the moon silvered the surface, refracting glistening explosions of light from the wave crests that leaped around us in crazy confusion. Somehow, this helped to make the night watches seem shorter than in the smothering dark, but it was still a long night before land, in the form of two islands, edged over the horizon off the port bow about 0800. They were supposed to be Virgin Gorda, with Necker Island just north of it, and if so, we were therefore surprisingly high of it, so we headed off to 250° to make Necker Island Passage.

As we got nearer, uninhabited "Necker Island" gradually exhibited quite a few houses, and "Virgin Gorda" was much more heavily settled than it was supposed to be. Some serious soul searching (and binocular viewing) made me admit that "Necker" had to be Buck Island and "Virgin Gorda" was St. Croix! In 14 hours of plodding through the lumpy seas we had been set almost 30 miles to the south by what must have been a strong and unusual current generated by the norther. Chalk up one more for Anegada Passage. Somewhat embarrassed, I turned on the engine at 1100 and headed directly into the wind for Norman Island, the southern-most British Virgin, still not visible to the north.

Now the norther began to ease, and it was reduced to a whisper when we poked into The Bight of Norman at 1600 to find the usual situation of about 50 boats at anchor in the deep cut that slices into Norman's uninhabited shores. The clear, slanting sunlight shone benignly on the scene of serenity, and at least there would not be the usual gusty tradewind puffs accelerating into The Bight through the gap in the hills at the head of the harbor. "Hashandpeassplendid" was the easiest solution to an early dinner, followed by very early bed. The norther's brisk authority and the lump of moonlit seas back in Anegada Passage seemed like some strange dream.

It was a night of flat calm, as the norther had blown itself completely out, and there was still no wind in the morning as we powered over a flat, shining Drake Channel to Virgin Gorda Yacht Harbour to enter the BVI formally. In contrast to our unforced routines of January, we now had several dates to keep, and the first was to do a piece for *Yachting* on a new Ocean 40 sloop. She had been built by our former son-in-law, Hank Hinckley, in his own brief venture into the same business as his father, and she was based at VGYH as part of a new scheme in yacht management, a time-share operation. (The scheme did not take.)

The marina was so busy that the only berth available was along the seawall on the west side of the basin, after apologies from Denise. It was a long walk all the way around the basin to the shore facilities, and it was too shallow even for our four-foot-nine draft. There can be a surge in the marina when there is a northerly swell, and there still was one left over from our recent maverick wind, so we spent an uneasy night bouncing on the bottom now and then. At first light, wide awake after a largely sleepless night, I spied a berth at one of the piers, opened up by an early departure, and we moved into it—Grumpy Grampy be damned.

After the sail and photo session with the Ocean 40, which took half a day, with normal tradewind weather back in business, we headed on to North

Sound in a fresh northeaster. The sky was the usual cumulus-flecked blue, the waves were a neat pattern of nicely-spaced whitecaps, and it was a day to remind us just how good BVI sailing can be, if we had ever forgotten.

There was also an exciting dividend. In the narrow section of Drake Passage between Colison Point and the collection of islands of scrub and rock called The Dogs, there was a disturbance in the water, and a great shadow took form and shape as a humpback whale, cruising slowly with a calf hovering close alongside. We had a fine view of them as they glided along, and Mama surfaced and blew a couple of times. It was a real thrill, but we did not want to get too close. It would be dangerous to arouse protective instincts, and wrong, of course, to upset them in any way. For about ten minutes we watched them swimming easily along, with the loom of the great shadow and its small satellite a dramatic contrast to the clear, transparent blue of the water. Then they veered off and disappeared.

Springtime and late winter are whale-sighting times in the Caribbean, and we have had the thrill of seeing them on several occasions, both down around the Grenadines and in the Virgins. Whale-sighting statistics are kept in the BVI, with a request for information to be phoned or radioed in to a special number, and reports are fairly numerous. Sometimes they are a surprise sight in rather confined waters. The news gets on the radio and people turn out in good numbers to watch from shore.

In addition to this mother and calf, we have seen the same combination right outside Road Town Harbour, and there have been reports of whales sporting around off the western end of Tortola for several days at a time. Whales are not hunted in this part of the world except for a vestigial, primitive operation out of Bequia in the northern Grenadines, where it is considered a banner year if one whale is caught. Bequians chase them down in primitive sailing dories, and they have a flensing station on a small off-island. Sailing to leeward of it one time, we had strong olfactory evidence that it had been a good year.

Dolphins (porpoises) are seldom seen in the protected waters of the Virgins, though they often frolic under a boat's bow in the open Caribbean. The same is true of flying fish, which are not seen in great numbers near the Virgins. Barbados is the flying fish "capital" of the area, where they are seen by the thousands, and there is a thriving commercial fishery of them. Their fillets are a tender treat.

Moving on to North Sound, we followed our usual tactic of jogging through the anchorage under main, sightseeing the boats while looking for a vacant Bitter End Yacht Club mooring. We finally spotted one and realized

Village Cay Marina

why it was vacant as we tried to pick it up—it had no pennant. It did have a ring, and we managed to get a line through it, to ride serenely through the night. At supper, I found that Neil was another guest who seemed to consider it a real privilege to be allowed to operate the hibachi (I came to think of this ploy of mine as the Tom Sawyer fence-painting act), and he did a fine job with the steaks as we settled down to tapes and chapeaux.

The next day, February 27th, happened to be our 39th wedding anniversary, and it turned out to be a fine one for celebration—one of those standard good BVI sailing days. There had been no rain over a calm night, and it was a bright, clear morning for setting sail, with the trades coming in properly, the hills of the islands shining in the early light, and the water colors over the reef at the entrance putting on their usual play of contrasts. We sailed out through the new American-style buoys (red, right, returning, in contrast to the opposite, which is the international standard everywhere else) that had just been placed in the cut through the reefs between Mosquito Island to the west and Prickly Pear to the east.

Feeling feisty on such a gorgeous morning for sailing we set the Flasher, which had had almost no use in the St. Martin area, and its multitude of colors, brilliant in the clear light, puffed proudly above us on a run in the open sea outside all the islands, until we rounded Great Camanoe. We went between it and Guana and into Trellis Bay, and finished off the gala day with a Last Resort evening that was up to the usual standards in food and Tony's performance. A last entry in my logbook was a rather wobbly "I drank too much."

We finished off the Lindemans' visit with a brisk sail to Cooper for lunch ashore and then on to Road Town and back home to Village Cay Marina. It was time for them to leave, and we got ready for our next "date." Part of my getting ready was in chores like cleaning the bilge, Nev-R-Dul, and washing the cockpit (a boatowner's work is never done!). Then we got together with the skippers of the crewed charterboats that were taking a group from the Princeton Club of New York on a cruise. As Chairman of the club's House Committee, which also ran the travel program, I had set up this rather unconventional club junket. We were to go along in *Brunelle* as part of the group.

There were three British yachts, *Jada*, *Chaucer*, and *Gypsy Dane*, operated respectively by Joe and Brigitte Joseph, Geoff and Marina Browning, and Barry and Roz Rice. They were all experienced charter people, with boats in the 50- to 60-foot range that were well set up and adapted to the trade. There were 18 Princetonians and companions of varying sorts equally divided among the boats. I had known some of them before—one from subchaser duty in New Guinea—and it was a modest sort of old-home week. They were all in a festive mood anticipating the cruise as we gathered for a get-together dinner at Robber Dick's Restaurant at Village Cay.

The cruise had been booked by a travel agency working with a yacht broker, and an itinerary had been set up for the seven days of sailing. The charter skippers and I went over plans, and we immediately, to a man, agreed that the schedule was nuts and unworkable. The distances were too long and criss-crossed the islands illogically, so we set up a plan that made much more sense. A couple of places had received advance deposits for dinner parties, and we naturally had to make them on schedule, but we fit them into a much smoother program.

Jane and I had been guests on crewed charters in the past, but this was the first time I had worked with professional crews on a cooperative basis, and it was a plus to get to know them this way. It ended up that they took their hard-won and infrequent relaxation by getting together with us in port when there was an opportunity, and we became good friends. We saw a lot of the Rices and Brownings particularly.

It was interesting to get to know crewed chartering from the other side of the picture, realizing how much continuous pressure the crews were under to keep things running smoothly, catering to charterers' often unreasonable and unpredictable whims, while hoping to avoid mechanical glitches and foul-ups. We were soon reminded of the truism that supposedly civilized, sophisticated people can become Grade-A horses' asses when paying to be catered to. One pair of female lawyers in the Princeton group had proved particularly hard to please, arbitrary and officious about almost everything, and they became the behind-the-back local joke of the charter crews. In general, though, things went very well, and fortunately the weather was lovely.

Our first stop was The Bight at Norman, with the side feature of dinghy exploration of the caves in the cliffs just south of the harbor, supposedly the inspiration for Robert Louis Stevenson's *Treasure Island,* and always a treat for charterers (except for those with an aversion to bats). The Bight is very popular, as noted, with 40 to 60 or more boats anchoring overnight, but it has some pitfalls. It is quite deep, and setting an anchor is difficult, especially because the usual tradewind gusts accelerate so forcefully as they funnel into the anchorage through the hills. To a newcomer, the northeast corner of the harbor looks like the best spot, as it is the shallowest and most protected part, but it is a snare and a delusion, as I found out when I first tried it. The bottom is grass on hard sand, and anchors do not like it. They can't dig in, and we dragged merrily out on our first visit. Since then, each time I have been there I have watched boats going through the same frustrating performance.

The night was calm, so much so that the anchored boats began to tend erratically on different headings. At 0600 I was awakened by the nudge of a CSY 44 on a very long scope that was tending the opposite way from us, but it was a light bump, with no harm done except to my sleep.

Although the night had been calm, a perfect breeze came in for the fleet to beat out between Norman and Peter, around Carrot Rock and into Cooper for lunch, and I got a kick out of staying ahead of the other boats. From there it was on to Marina Cay for one of our pre-paid dinners. It turned out to be a very good one, with everyone in a party mood, in the newly-opened waterfront restaurant. The famous hammock, I noted, was still hanging between the trees by the beach.

The calm came back overnight, a welcome development at Marina Cay, as a good breeze can push a surge over the protecting reef at high tide. Tide range in the BVI is about two feet, or less, but even this range could make a difference here. The reef used to be great for snorkeling, but Hurricane David the previous year had torn up and killed its coral heads. The calm persisted, forcing us to power to the next rendezvous at Drake's Anchorage in North Sound.

The trades came back again over the next night, just right for the special highlight of the week, a 14-mile sail north to Anegada. Anegada is an anomaly in the Virgins, a low, sandy island more like a Bahamian cay, with beautiful beaches, scrub vegetation, an encirclement of reefs excellent for diving, a tiny native settlement, and one informal inn and restaurant. It is off limits to bareboats because of the reefs, and therefore a special treat for crewed boats. We had been wanting to get up there but had never worked out the time, so this was a treat for us too.

It was a perfect day for the passage, with a moderate trade on the beam and the sun playing upon the variations in water color from the changing depths over the bottom, generally quite shallow for the whole way. A couple of Princeton Club visitors came with us for a "sailing lesson," and it was an ideal time for them to take the wheel and get the feel of the boat as she reached smoothly along. Although this area seems like the open sea, it is separated from Anegada Passage by a long string of reefs, notorious through the years for shipwrecks, and therefore popular now for diving. Booby birds swooped around us, skimming the surface in graceful flight, and this was, again, obviously the whale season, as we saw one flipping its flukes and blowing, partway to the horizon.

The approach to the anchorage off the hotel is through a maze of reefs marked by posts, and you are supposed to line up Jost Van Dyke directly on your stern, but, 25 miles away, it was obscured in haze. I thought I had observed the posts correctly on the way in, only to have the hotel manager question me when I went ashore. "How the hell did you ever come in that way? You missed one turn in the channel, and you should have gone aground."

He had been trying to call me on VHF to warn me, but I had not had the radio on. He thought we had the six-foot draft of the standard CSY 37s, but I explained that we had the shallow draft version, and that had been just enough to get us safely in.

Later in the afternoon, a flotilla of half a dozen 26-foot Maxis, a Swedish design, escorted by a mother ship, came into the anchorage and put on a spectacular show of how not to anchor. Flotilla cruising is a European phenomenon that had recently been introduced into the Virgins, and this was a good example of why they needed a mother ship. One of them finally came to rest so close alongside us that I practically could have helped myself to hors d'oeuvres from their cocktail table. The people aboard were non-English-speaking Scandinavians of some variety, who tried to ignore my questioning gestures as they settled down for schnapps, but they finally got the word and moved off resentfully for another half-hour exercise.

With their passengers ashore, *Gypsy Dane* invited us for dinner, and if it was an example of their usual fare, their guests had been doing very well. We had a pleasant time watching the Rices in their chance to relax. Soft-spoken and seemingly the epitome of British reserve, they livened up, and the sea stories and tales of chartering adventures flowed easily.

During the night, the wind played a dirty trick, swinging around to the south, a wide open bearing at Anegada, and an extremely rare occurrence. The anchorage became very lumpy, waking us up early. The flotilla boats were bouncing around and dragging all over the place, with their shepherd from the mothership dashing madly about in a dinghy trying to give advice and directions. We decided to get the hell out of there after a quick breakfast. We powered out through the stakes without incident, and, despite the fact that it's practically illegal to have to beat back to Virgin Gorda from Anegada, we had a fine sail, making Mosquito Island in two long tacks at 1215. Again we saw whales, and this time much closer to us. One put on a fantastic show of vertical leaps, tail completely clear of the water and the sun gleaming on the white of the belly, to land back in explosive splashes, evidently a form of mating dance. I hope the female was as impressed as we were.

We kept on for Trellis Bay, the rendezvous of the night, where we entertained the Rices for cocktails, and then everyone went ashore after dinner for Tony's show. Most enjoyed it in a gala mood, but the lady lawyers, difficult as ever, did not. Sexist? Lewd? Too British? Who knows.

The finale of the cruise was the other prepaid dinner, this time at Peter Island Yacht Club. Things had gone so well that the law of averages caught up here: *Chaucer* had gearbox trouble and anchored outside of tiny Sprat Bay in Great Harbour, and *Jade's* transmission failed while she was making a landing at the marina where we were berthed. Fortunately, dock lines were already over and prevented a smash arrival.

Our men had to, horror of horrors, don jacket and tie for dinner at the hotel dining room (the roast beef was rather tough), where dancing to a calypso band was the entertainment. The cook from *Jade*, a very shapely young woman, tanned to a native-brown hue and clad in a minimum of mini-dress, was the hit of the party, putting on quite a show of dancing with all and sundry. Somehow, at one point, I ended up dancing with four women at once. The lady lawyers remained aloof.

The end of this unusual affair marked a "spring break" for us, as we had to fly home for a couple of weeks of miserable March in New Jersey while I worked on my income tax and played in a couple of squash tournaments. (The local doubles championship is named for me, and I claim to be one of the few people who plays in his own "memorial" tournament.) We would be back on *Brunelle* by April 1, though, with many more adventures to contemplate.

13

NEW HORIZONS

IN LOOKING BACK over the previous three months, which now seemed to have flown by in the wink of an eye, I had no regrets and many good memories. There had been much more excitement than I had ever imagined; of course I could have done without water in the fuel, the surge in Philipsburg, French yachts anywhere near us, mechanical failures, and the conditions in Anegada Passage, but they added up to "experience," and all in all it had been one of the most rewarding times we had ever spent afloat.

Now we would be into quite a different operation. Instead of our own decisions on cruising routines, I had assignments from *Yachting* that had to be met, specifically to cover CORT, a new ocean racing event that was in its second season. CORT is an acronym (and what would we do without acronyms?) for Caribbean Ocean Racing Triangle, putting three events together in a series leading to an overall championship, somewhat like that other acronym event, the SORC (Southern Ocean Racing Conference) in Florida and the Bahamas at that time.

The three events in CORT were the Rolex Regatta in St. Thomas, USVI; the BVI Spring Regatta in Tortola, and Antigua Race Week. They were all in the month of April, and they would keep us hopping under a much different kind of routine. There would be no geriatric quartets, trios, or duos, as we needed younger crew to help us move around, and, heaven forgive me, race. Yes, we would actually be entering some of the competition. I had never figured on racing in any of my planning for *Brunelle*, and she was not set up at all as a racing boat. But there were cruising-class divisions in the regattas, and the people involved with running them had worked on my sense of sportsmanship to persuade me to enter.

Over the years, I had had to take part in a lot of ocean racing, covering events for *Yachting*. Actually taking part in them was often the best way to do coverage, and, in my position at the magazine, I had to feign enthusiasm for this phase of sailing, whether I really liked it or not. I will admit that some of the experiences were fun and exciting, especially the unique fellowship there is in an ocean racing crew, and it took me to Bermuda, the Bahamas, the Caribbean, the Greek Islands, the Baltic, the Kattegat and Skagerrak, and the top sailing spots in North America. Two Bermuda races gave me enough background on that event to allow me to retire to the Race Committee from then on, which I did for 36 years. This gave me the "big picture," including airplane surveys of the race in progress as press pool representative.

With all this, I had some basic objections to ocean racing, or more particularly, handicap racing. I did not dislike racing *per se*, and we raced our catboat on the Shrewsbury for many years. That was one-design racing, which to me is the only satisfying kind. When you finish ahead of another boat, you know that you have beaten it, and it is a rewarding form of "hand-to-hand" combat. There are very few excuses that can be made if you are beaten in a one-design race.

In handicap racing, however, which is what ocean racing almost always is, there are all sorts of opportunities to make excuses. First of all, to my mind there has never been a thoroughly satisfactory rating rule for working out handicaps ever since the first one in England in 1807. There is always a chance to bitch about the fact that the rule favors big boats, or small boats, or that it is only good in light air, or heavy air. There has never been a rule that a knowledgeable naval architect could not "beat" with an artful design, and often, the best way to beat a rule has been to produce an "unnatural" boat—unseaworthy, cranky, and uncomfortable. This was certainly the case with the IOR (International Offshore Rule) that was in vogue in the '70s and '80s, and almost wrecked the sport.

We had raced *Mar Claro* fairly often, as this was the era when my taking part was politically wise. She was a good, fast performer, and we won our share with her, but I still did not get a great kick out of beating a boat on time allowance if the crew was already well on the way to getting drunk in the bar by the time we finished. I still liked to look back and see the boat we were beating astern of us. I can't remember being in a handicap race when there were no complaints about how the rule had been unfair to someone.

We also raced *Tanagra* a few times, including a "regatta" our local Morgan dealer used to put on for boats of that make, and it was, I admit, great fun to beat Out Island 41s with our OI 36. We also entered the cruising class on the New York Yacht Club cruise a couple of times, just to be along for the spectacle and festivities, and I set my own standards there. If we were not last boat-for-boat, or at the bottom of the printed results list, we had "won," and we thereby managed to "win" every day. There was even one fine day when, by playing the tides right in Vineyard Sound, we beat two Hinckley Pilots boat-for-boat, which I reported to our then son-in-law with great glee.

Another objection I had to ocean racing was the fact that you had to go to sea at a specific time. This feeling stemmed from my Navy days, when orders would read "When in all respects ready for sea, you will depart 0900," come rain, snow, hell, or high water. This always made work out of going to sea, and it lent the same feeling to racing in which, no matter how nasty the weather, there was an established starting time. In cruising, it is very rare to have to leave port at a specific hour, which is one of its charms for me.

Now, here I was agreeing to race, but I looked on this as a one-off situation, governed by sportsmanship (and public relations). Poor *Brunelle* would just have to suffer through it.

Our flight down after our New Jersey break was standard, with the connection from San Juan to Beef Island on Air BVI this time, following the established tradition of being 45 minutes late. When we got to Village Cay, there were bubbles surfacing around *Brunelle*'s waterline. Peter Clarke was under the hull with scuba, cleaning it. He was just then in the middle of the work list I had left two weeks ago when we went home, which is standard BVI procedure and is known as "island time." As usual, though, the work he did was good, and he managed to have the list complete by the time we were ready to set sail the next morning.

Our crew arrived soon after we did. This time it was Jim Lillie and a companion, Beverly Lee, a slender, appealing Chinese girl. Jim was now a *Brunelle* regular, as this was his third time with us. In 1979, when I was planning to bring *Brunelle* down to the Caribbean from the builder's yard in Tampa, he had come in to the *Yachting* office in New York looking for a chance to get in some sailing. A recent graduate of Wesleyan, he was not yet set on what career moves to make—possibly law school—and had decided to see more of the world first. He had spent some time backpacking in Europe, and he was eager to continue the nomadic life for a time longer.

A handsome, six-foot redhead with a rather shy manner but a ready smile, he had been brought up in a sailing family and guaranteed he was not into "controlled substances," so I signed him on, and he turned out to be an ideal crewmember. He had joined us in the Caicos for the rest of the passage to the BVI, when we were most in need of a good crew, and then had been with us the next season for the last month of sailing.

He was very self-sufficient, read a lot, made quite a project out of studying the stars at night, and never seemed bored to be cooped up in 37 feet with people old enough to be his grandparents. When in port, he did a lot of exploring on his own, and he also was good at making friends with people his own age on other boats. We were delighted to have him back, and Beverly, though not an experienced sailor, was thoroughly charming and fit in easily.

They helped Jane with some shopping while I went to clear out at Customs and Immigration, and Peter Clarke finished up the jobs he had been doing. We were loaded with fuel, water, and propane, and ready for a new approach to setting sail from Road Town—turning to starboard. The breeze was as usual as we powered out of Village Cay at 1130 and set main and staysail for the run west in Drake Channel. We hung out the staysail with a preventer and rolled our way toward The Narrows, where Drake Channel ends and St. John and the islands that string westward from Tortola, Little and Great Thatch, are less than a mile apart. It was easy sailing, with *Brunelle* doing her usual pendulum act, but not too wildly, and the sun on the mountains, the salt-scented trades, and the play of whitecaps over the deep blue of Drake Channel made us very glad to be back.

St. John is almost as high as Tortola, with Bordeaux Mountain close to 1300 feet and several other peaks over 1000. Its hills are gracefully contoured, and there is a natural, unspoiled look to it as most of it is National Park, a donation from the Rockefellers. A few ruined sugar mills can be seen in the hills, and the vegetation is a rich, tropical mix, unbroken by buildings over most of the island. There are several good harbors and beaches, and St. John is a dramatic contrast to St. Thomas, its neighbor just to the west, which is a teeming shambles, overbuilt and overcrowded, with all the bad features that go with the term "tourist trap." St. Thomas does have impressive hills, pleasant beaches, and several good harbors, but there could not be a stronger contrast in atmosphere than there is between these neighbors. They are classic examples of how to and how not to handle naturally endowed areas.

Fortunately, the current, which is always strong in The Narrows, was with us, and it was a smooth slide past Leinster Bay, the easternmost anchorage on St. John's north side, where several boats were at anchor. If the current is heading east against the trades, it can kick up a steep, short chop in these confined waters. At the very narrowest, between steeply hilly Great Thatch and the sheer bluff on Mary Point, 578 feet high, on St. John, we started to head more to the southwest, past rugged little Whistling Cay, separated from Mary Point by a narrow cut into the excellent anchorage at Francis Bay. This is one of the best protected harbors in all the Virgins, with a white curve of beach at its head, and ringed with hills. It is the most popular stop in the USVI, and there is always a good gathering of boats there.

We had one amusing memory of Francis Bay from our 1964 *Circe* cruise. Above the beach, high on a steep hill, a house had been built for a rather elderly woman who was a writer. The construction was accomplished by having all the materials carried up the steep slope by donkeys, which evidently made for some colorful complications. She produced a book about the experience, sort of a *Mr. Blanding's Dream House* type of thing, and she sent it in to her publishers. They accepted it but made her change the title, which she thought was very unreasonable of them. What was her title? *I Did It With Donkeys.*

Our skipper on *Circe* was an excellent relaxer at the bar, and he indulged well at a party we all went to at the "donkey house," so well that, when it was time to leave via the precipitous path back down to the beach, he suddenly took off into space like a ski jumper, with a strangled cry following him down in a diminishing wail. We fully expected to find his body in a heap at the bottom, but there he was, halfway down the slope, dusting himself off and continuing on his way at a slightly slower but still unsteady pace, acting as though nothing had happened.

St. John would be a more attractive, and frequent, target for us except for the nuisance of having to cross the international boundary. You should formally check out and enter Customs and Immigration in each place, which takes time, and a bit of money, and for that reason we hardly ever went there despite its obvious attractions. Occasionally we would duck over and anchor in Leinster or Francis, with no intention of going ashore. A U.S. flag vessel would not ordinarily be questioned, but the possibility of a snafu was always there, hanging a bit of a cloud over the visit. It was silly to feel guilty and illegal in your own national territory, but there it was.

One time when we were in Leinster for the night on just such a visit, I pumped the bilge on getting up, a daily reflex action, and, as usual, and inevitably, there was a tiny trace of oil in what I had pumped. We were then eating breakfast in the cockpit when a U.S. Park Ranger launch, which had been making the rounds of all the anchored boats, came alongside, and the starchily uniformed Ranger, in the best officer-of-the-law manner, said, "Somebody pumped their bilge and got oil in the water here. Please be advised that it is an illegal act."

Ready to hide my head under a pillow, I merely nodded and acknowledged the message with a subdued "Thank you," and the boat moved on. All St. John's harbors are under this kind of control, and proper behavior is a must. Fortunately, I was not actually pumping when he made his rounds, and I had shamefacedly learned a lesson.

Next after Francis Bay came several small bays that are all good anchorages. Cinnamon Bay is tucked into the southwest corner of Francis Bay, and next is Trunk Bay, site of an underwater diving trail that is a great favorite with snorkelers of all grades from beginner to expert. It lies off a graceful, palm-lined beach which is backed by steeply rising, 1000-foot hills. Over a clear sand bottom, the trail is easily followed and well-marked, with a succession of coral heads and small reefs, all identified by signs, and it displays most of the standard underwater flora and fauna of the area. Tame and well-organized as it is, it is still a treat, and well worth doing.

The bay is a fine anchorage except in a northerly surge, when ocean-caliber breakers can sweep in from the open bearing out to the Atlantic in the north. There is another special feature at Trunk Bay—Johnson Reef, large and circular, covering over half a mile in diameter, just north of the anchorage. Even the lightest surge breaks on it, causing a continuous boil that is easily visible, and it is marked by buoys on the north and south. It is a very obvious, easily identified hazard, but it is amazing how many times we have seen boats stranded on it.

We swept by its northern buoy, noting a good boil over the partly exposed lumps of the reef, then went on past Hawksnest and Caneel Bay, threading our way between small lumps of rock called the Durloe Cays off Hawksnest Point.

Caneel Bay is the site of the original Caribbean Rock Resort, whose buildings are spread over many acres of manicured hillsides, connected by winding roads, with a choice of several very special beaches, and a good harbor that is usually full of boats. It is a place where living in casual luxury is raised to the nth degree, in a setting that is letter perfect.

Now headed southwest, with St. Thomas and its hillsides speckled with buildings looming ever larger to starboard, we ducked around the point into Cruz Bay to enter U.S. Customs and Immigration. Cruz Bay is the major settlement on St. John, in fact the only one except for a couple of tiny ones at Hurricane Hole at the east end. The only part of St. John that is not national park is the area around Cruz Bay, and each year we have seen it become more touristy and crowded, but the atmosphere is still light years away from St. Thomas. The anchorage is small and very crowded, and there is continuous ferry traffic in the narrow main channel to the ferry dock. We managed to anchor a short dinghy row from the dock, and the red tape and paperwork were quickly and efficiently handled. We have never spent any more time in Cruz Bay than it takes to clear in or out, as it is a much too busy and crowded spot for relaxing.

The wind had gone fluky, so we powered the short run across to the narrow slit of Current Cut between St. James Island and the southeast tip of St. Thomas, leading directly into Cowpet Bay. This had become the home anchorage of the very active St. Thomas Yacht Club some 20 years previously, and its small semicircle, ringed in hills that hold row on row of condominiums, was absolutely jammed with boats. I wondered what we could do about coming to rest in this incredible jumble of boats, when the club launch came along, and we were directed to the "Fischer mooring." An empty mooring was pointed out, and we picked it up, happy to have a solution. We had barely settled down when a sloop came alongside, steered by Dick Avery, the salty New Englander who had established the original yacht yard in St. Thomas many years before, where we had based on our 1966 bareboat cruise. He had a purposeful scowl on his face, probably the way I look when approaching trespassers on the CCA mooring in Little Harbour, then did a double-take when he recognized me.

"Oh—Hi, Bill. Ah—how come you're on that mooring?"

"Hi, Dick. The club launch told us to. Why?"

"Well. It's mine."

It was my turn to do a double-take, and I started to make apologetic noises. "Sorry, Dick. They told me it was Fischer's."

"That's what they think." He held up a hand in a stop signal and started looking around the anchorage, then pointed. "That's Fischer's," he said, indicating another empty one. "What the hell. I'll take that one."

With a cheerful wave he moved on to it.

Perhaps I should have been warned that this might be an indication of disorganization to come, but they were perfectly organized to take my $75 registration fee when I rowed ashore to the attractive, modern clubhouse and was told that the skippers' meeting for the Rolex Regatta was at 1800. *Brunelle*'s new career had officially begun.

14

ONE LEG OF A TRIANGLE

THE ANCHORAGE, WITH the sun streaming across it as it lowered in the west, was a vibrant scene of activity. Almost every boat had people aboard, gathered in the cockpit over anchor cups, or moving around on deck tuning rigging and checking gear. It would seem that not even a kayak could fit into the mooring area any more, but boats kept coming in, the sun reflecting in bursts off their aluminum masts, and somehow they all found a place to raft up or drop a hook.

Next to us was a sleek J/36 ketch named *Blue Bayou*, a hot racer. She had a loudspeaker on the mast that kept playing the song by that name, and I have to admit to rather dense reactions in not realizing the phonetic significance of the name for a racing boat. I guess I was still back with Benny Goodman and Glenn Miller.

I left the rest of the crew aboard and headed for the 1800 skippers' meeting, to find the trim clubhouse, usually pleasantly roomy on normal days, a seething madhouse of sailors jammed in like a rush hour crowd in the Times Square subway station. With close to 100 boats racing, and four or more per crew, it made a good crowd. There was a strong aura of sweat and beer, as almost everyone (the group was 80 percent male) was clutching a can, and the decibel level was way up there. It flashed back to me what this reminded me of: It was like the bar at the Officers' Club in Noumea, New Caledonia, in October 1943, which, at the time, was the busiest Navy base in the South Pacific. The nightly gathering there, with a great number of ships in the harbor, had been a frenetic mob scene, where you had to bring your own containers to get a drink.

That was not the case here, but everyone did have a can or glass in hand, and the noisy reunions between sailing friends, the exchange of sea stories, and general banter hit a tremendous noise level. After a Mount Gay or two to loosen me up, I was right in the thick of it, with lots of sailing friends to tip glasses with. Dick Avery and I bumped into each other and had a laugh over the mooring mixup.

The skippers' meeting, with announcements and instructions the order of the agenda, was finally called to "order" at 1930. Very little of what was announced got through the crowd noise, but I did get two salient facts: The cruising division, composed of the slowest boats in the fleet, was scheduled as the last to start at 1030, and it had the same length course as the racing boats, 31 miles. It was also announced that no finishes would be recorded after an 1800 deadline. This made no sense to me, as, first of all, the cruising division would have a hard time finishing that long a course in that time, and second, if one boat in a class did finish before the deadline, all the boats in her class should be given a finish. This is standard racing procedure, and it was especially important since the regatta was part of CORT, and scores would be counted over all three regattas for the series championship.

It happened that two old shipmates of mine were running the race committee—John Nichols and Art Wullschleger. John had built up a reputation internationally as a race official and made a career of it. He and I had sailed together in a couple of Long Island Sound races. He also had been foredeck boss on the 12-Meter *American Eagle* in the 1964 America's Cup trials when our son Robby had been a winch grinder. I had always gotten along well with him, and Robby was a great admirer.

Art Wullschleger and I had been fellow crewmembers in several SORC campaigns in Jack Brown's *Calloh*, and there was one incident we would not forget. He was the navigator, and he always smoked a potent cigar as he worked at the nav station. I suppose it was a symbol of toughness, but it was also tough on the stomach of shipmates in the Gulf Stream. He loved to put on a gruff "don't bother me" act while he was working, but I had to bother him when I came off watch halfway across the Gulf Stream in a Miami–Nassau Race, because the bunk I had been assigned was under the nav table, which slanted over it.

As I hoisted myself into it while he impatiently hooked the table over me again so he could get back to his figures, I said, "How do you get out of this thing?"

"Shut up and go to sleep" was his smoke-blown answer. "We'll get you out when it's your watch."

Before my watch, however, *Calloh* took a knockdown on a spinnaker broach, and I was suddenly wakened tossing around in the bunk with all sense of up-and-down gone. I could hear water pouring into the cabin, and for all I knew we had done a 180. I started scrabbling at the hooks of the confining nav table, with no idea how to work them, yelling "Get me out of here!" No one came, and I finally figured out how to escape from what I thought might be my nautical coffin. It turned out that it had been a normal broach, not a capsize, and the water I had heard was from a port that had carelessly been left open over the galley. By the time I came topsides, everything was under control, and I caught a lot of flak about missing an "all hands on deck." Since then, Art and I have had many a laugh over my predicament.

Now I went to him and John as an old friend and shipmate, and as a frequent member of race committees myself, and complained about the 1800 cutoff, especially since the slowest boats were to start last.

"That's the way it is," was the curt answer. "We don't want to stay out there all night."

"How about the CORT standings?" I asked.

"Tough luck. If you don't make it, you don't make it."

Nothing I said could change them, and I left under a last blast of Art's cigar smoke. By the time I got back to *Brunelle* from this shambles, Jane, Jim and Bev had had dinner, figuring I must have had something to eat on shore by then, and I had to scrabble up a sandwich. At least it was a clear, pleasant evening.

It remained the same for the start the next morning, and, being in the last class to start, I had plenty of time to take pictures to go with my article for *Yachting.* Years ago, when I was a newspaper boating writer on the *Newark News,* they would not let a reporter take photos, and I always had to have one of the dozen staff photographers with me when the assignment required one. Then I switched to the *Newark Star-Ledger,* whose entire photo staff was two overworked men, and I was told I had to take my own art. I was given a Minolta Autocord, and directed to use it myself. The only advice was "Film is cheap. Take lots of shots, and one might turn out OK."

I had done more and more photography ever since. Film was no longer that cheap, as I was shooting color, but the theory still applied: maybe one in 50 would be usable. I had even found this to be true in going through the files of the famous marine photographer Rosenfeld's agency, looking for a shot I wanted. Here was the top man in the field, a genius with a camera, and there were lots of unusable shots.

So I clicked away and enjoyed the starts, as each class went on its way. One of the best times for action photos, the start is a wonderful time of

Brunelle

building excitement. With several minutes to go until the gun, the boats mill about in seemingly aimless fashion, but gradually, as the seconds tick away, their actions become more organized until they climax in the last frantic minute. Then the jumble coalesces into a pattern, with all boats purposefully aiming at the starting line, and there is a great concerted whoosh, with everyone tight together and concentrating madly. Tension hums through the fleet, and a sense of frantic urgency takes over, which is almost unique to a sail race start, though to some it might seem like the first collision of bodies after the kickoff in a football game. Cries and shouts mix with the sounds of wakes clashing, sails being trimmed, and, sometimes, hulls bumping. Then the gun goes off and they are away, leaving a froth of wakes and a diminishing echo of sounds behind.

When it became our turn at the mad rush, I put the camera away and got a fairly good start, but it was not long before my basic feelings about *Brunelle* as a racing boat were confirmed. Ideally rigged for toughing out brisk tradewind cruising conditions, she was under-rigged for racing. The double-head rig was efficient for cruising to windward, but a big genoa would naturally be faster. We were one of the smallest boats in the class, and boats that started behind us were soon charging by and blanketing us. By the first windward mark there was only one boat behind us, and she soon disappeared, leaving us more and more alone as the 31-mile course to The Narrows and around Great Thatch dragged on. Since it was a non-spinnaker class, we could not use the Flasher on the runs, and our small sail area really told.

As the afternoon wore on, I began to wonder about the 1800 deadline, and there was one somewhat satisfying thought: at least we would be keeping Art and John out there to the limit of their duty on the committee boat. I relished imagining the remarks they were making about me as the only boat still on the course.

The breeze was fading with the daylight, and it was not exactly a thrilling ride as we drifted toward the line in the bay outside Current Cut, eyes on our watches as the seconds ticked away toward the magic hour. Finally, we made it, but not until 18:01:56, and I gleefully saluted my friend and called, "Have you had a nice day?"

They already had the anchor halfway up, and made rude gestures at me in return. So our racing debut was a "Did Not Finish."

The "entertainment" at the club that night was a barbecue, and, if possible, it was more crowded and more of a shambles than the skippers' meeting, with sailors standing in long lines, empty plates impatiently slapping at their thighs, waiting to be served. Bev and Jim managed to mix in and have fun, but I was soon back on board, where Jane had wisely remained.

The weather turned overnight, with more wind and heavy rain. We had had to raft with another boat on the mooring, and the new conditions, stirring everyone around in the crowded harbor, put us perilously close to the next raft. There was not much that could be done except put fenders out, but I sat in the cockpit watching things for over an hour in the pre-dawn darkness in case fenders had to be used. Close but no cigar, in an anxious, and wet, watch.

The dawn was bleak, not an appealing prospect for racing, and I soon decided we would have a "lay-day." This turned out to be a wise move, as the day remained stormy, with gusts in the 30s, and the fleet took a beating. There were several dismastings, one small boat capsized, broaches were a dime a dozen, and torn sails and gear failures were everywhere. A great many boats dropped out, as we sat smugly in port.

The evening's schedule called for a reception for the press and officials at the Danish Consulate in Charlotte Amalie, a building dating from 1830, when Denmark owned the Virgin Islands. High on a hill above the city, it had a sweeping view of the lights below, but the atmosphere was period European, not tropical, with dark, heavy furniture (and rapidly disappearing, fancy hors d'oeuvres). Afterwards, some of the press and local committee had dinner at a hotel called The 1829, which supposedly had a top grade menu, but the service was slow and the food (I had medallions of veal) only so-so. I finally struggled back on board at 0100.

It was still rainy and squally in the morning, but I decided to be a sport and go in the last race. With more wind, we did a better job of staying with the fleet. The cruising class had boats like the Cal 40, which not too long before had been classed as a hot racing machine, but we were up there with the fleet and having fun when we got to the first mark. A long run dropped us back, and we settled into a personal duel with *Taurus*, a 42-foot sloop, as the day wore on. The squalls and rain got nastier, and boat after boat dropped out, while we plugged away with the rain in our face. At least it is a warm rain in this part of the world.

At one point, it was blowing over 40 in a gusty squall. We were doing fine under full main and staysail, but, looking around, I realized that we were the only boat left. Everyone near us had quit, so we joined the DNFs and were back on the mooring by 1600.

As the shambles to top all the shambles of the weekend, the trophy dinner was a mammoth affair at the huge Frenchman's Reef Hotel. The self-congratulatory speeches went on and on in the sprawling expanse of the banquet hall, and no matter what was said, the words were lost on us. We were parked at a pair of tables way off in a corner, whose other occupants were two Puerto Rican crews, who had their own noisy party in Spanish, paying no attention to the formal program (I couldn't blame them, really).

Thus ended our first excursion into racing with a DNS, two DNFs, and three shambles. *Brunelle* was not going to be subjected to the indignity of having to race any more, but there were two-thirds of the triangle of CORT still to cover.

15

THE RIGHT KIND OF RACING

WITH THE ROLEX Regatta ended, the weather obligingly cleared up for our return to a cruising mode, and we had a "first" on our return to Tortola: south-about St. John. We had never been on its Caribbean side, and, with a fresh northeaster under the smiling-again sky, the water was smooth in the lee. We close-reached easily along the succession of tempting harbors that slice into its hills: Great Cruz Bay, Chocolate Hole, Rendezvous Bay, Fish Bay, and Lameshur Bay, with occasional stretches of beach in between. Lameshur Bay's Beehive Cove, on its eastern side, was the site of a U.S. Navy experimental program called Tektite, in which aquanauts lived for days, and even weeks, at a time in sealabs 50 feet down, observing sea life and testing the conditions and stresses of individuals living under water.

It was a scenic sail, with the empty blue reaches of the Caribbean to starboard and St. Croix's humped profile on the horizon on the starboard quarter. Each bay had its allure, but it was too early, and we kept going along the six-mile stretch to Salt Pond Bay at the southeast tip, tucked under Bordeaux Mountain and the 1000-foot Minna Hill.

We had never been there before. The Yachtsman's Guide touted it as an excellent anchorage, which it is. A big, very noticeable reef straddles the entrance, and once inside there is a good holding ground in clear white sand off a gem of a beach. The Park Service had established a picnic area at the beach, with tables and garbage cans, but it still had an away-from-it-all feeling. With only a couple of other boats sharing it, it was the least crowded anchorage we had been in in a long time—certainly a contrast to a Cowpet Bay's cheek-to-jowl crunch.

Bev and Jim went snorkeling on the reef right away. They reported that it was excellent, and they also poked around on the beach. A Nicholson 32 with a home port of Saginaw, Michigan, came in, and the attractive couple aboard, Judy and Frank Blessing, came over to say hello, introducing themselves as friends of CSY-owner friends of ours. We asked them aboard for a drink, it being that time of day. He was a telephone company lineman who had had an on-the-job injury that had forced a retirement at an early age, and the compensation from it had allowed them four years of cruising from the Great Lakes to Europe and back, with lots of interesting adventures—an unusual "blue collar" retirement.

We had one inconvenience as a result of all the rain during the Rolex. One item that had not been up to standard in CSY's construction was pot metal for drain pipes for the scuppers in the little well-deck areas just forward of the cockpit. The starboard one had corroded through, swamping the pots-and-pans compartment in the galley and putting the stove out of commission by flooding the LPG control switch. This meant that the hibachi, under Jim's ministration, had to come to the rescue for cooking the chops, and we had a one-burner propane stove for heating the peas. Bev glamorized the chops with a special marinade sauce, so we hardly suffered, and it was an early-to-bed night after a few music tapes.

Bev and Jim were up early, exploring ashore around the salt pond just behind the beach that gave the harbor its name, and they said that there wasn't much to see. We had a leisurely mid-morning start for a fine sail, tacking through Flanagan Passage, with a short sightsee into the Hurricane Hole complex that chops the east end of St. John into several well-protected harbors. It actually lives up to its name and is a good hurricane hole. The only drawback for it as a routine cruising stop is the likelihood of an excess of flies and mosquitoes, something the ever-efficient Park Service has not solved.

The breeze was fresh northeast as we beat our way past Flanagan Island, the last outpost of U.S. territory between St. John and Norman Island, and on across the whitecapped blue of Drake Channel, under a scattering of tradewind clouds, to CSY in Road Harbour. There we went right to work getting new scupper pipes of better material installed, and the LPG switch was replaced. Also, a great triumph, we were finally able to get three replacement springs for the hatches. These were a special design of which CSY was very proud that popped the hatches up and then braced them firmly. They were a wonderful innovation except that they did break. No replacement had been available for months, but now there was a new supply.

The dilemma over sparing *Brunelle* the indignation of racing was solved when Simon Scott, Manager of CSY, invited me to skipper a CSY 44 in the

BVI Regatta, as half a dozen were taking part as a one-design class within the cruising division, and the more the merrier. No CSY 37s were entered. This was a wonderful solution, and I accepted happily.

There were two days before the first race, so to give Bev and Jim some action, we zipped over to Little Harbour on a very fast reach in a strong northeaster. While Jane and I read and napped, they snorkeled along the shore with satisfying results and a visit with Corinne Chubb's pet barracuda. The return sail in the afternoon was hard on the wind, with a short hitch to make it into Road Harbour. It was amazing how the "Christmas Winds" had become "Easter Winds," but Christmas still got the blame. In cruising conditions like this, *Brunelle* usually outsailed nearby boats in her size range, but I now realized, after her racing debut, that this had something to do with the way the other boats were being sailed, and with the quality of the sails on charterboats.

Jane had developed a feverish cold and went to bed, so I took Bev and Jim to The Cloud Room for dinner, and it was an experiential and culinary success as usual, with the added excitement of skidding into a ditch on the ride down. It was a quick reaction from Paul Wattley, driving our bus, to avoid a collision with a Lincoln Continental, too big for these roads, and fortunately the ditch was a shallow one. No harm done.

A rainy, blowy day followed while we holed up at Village Cay for shopping and puttering and the arrival of John Yeoman (minus Santa suit) and his friend Aimee. The skippers' meeting was at the BVI Yacht Club's small headquarters in a bar at The Fort Burt Hotel atop a steep hill overlooking the harbor entrance. It was a condensed version of the Rolex shambles, as more than 60 boats were registered and instructions were handed out. Still, there was a better orderliness to it despite the decibels of crowd noise in the jammed room. A sense of anticipation was heightened by a strong, cloud-freighted northeaster gusting through the doors that opened onto a terrace over the harbor, with two bulky black cannons, relics of when this was a fort in colonial days, standing ineffectual guard, mostly covered by grass.

The breeze was even stronger in the morning as I transferred to my new command, the CSY 44 *Voyager I*. I knew the 44 well, as we had sailed on No. 1 back in 1977, writing it up for *Yachting,* and we had cruised in one in the Bay Islands of Honduras. They are sturdy, heavily built boats, slightly under-rigged for the same reason as the 37, being intended for tradewind charter cruising. They are capable sailers, not speed demons. But they would be fine for one-design racing. Jim, Bev and Jane took off to spend the day in Little Harbour in *Brunelle*. Jane's cold was better.

My crew consisted of John and Aimee, a native hand from the CSY staff, and Robert Large, a happy-go-lucky young Limey who was a waiter-bartender jack-of-all-trades at The Last Resort. Except for John, sailing experience was practically nil, but there are not a lot of demands on the crew in a spinnaker-less cruising division boat. The CSY lad and Robert had never raced before, and they were bug-eyed with excitement as we headed for the 0930 start. Fortunately, BVI Yacht Club's race committee, headed by Albie Stewart of Tortola Yacht Services, was smart enough to start the slower classes first, unlike at the Rolex. Actually, with the amount of wind that was piling in from the northeast, it didn't look as if there would be any problem with going over the time limit.

The start favored port tack, and we squeezed out a good one, high on the line. We had everyone but two Cal 39s, admittedly faster boats, tucked away by the first mark, but we had no pole to wing out the genoa on the downwind leg and we lost some ground to Simon Scott, who just happened to have a pole in his boat. We soon stopped worrying about any other boats but the CSYs. We found that a reefed main was best on windward legs, as the breeze kept its weight all day, and we were finished by 1440. The solid CSY 44 workhorses were right at home in this kind of air. Our finish was slightly blighted by my fouling the entrance buoy at Road Harbour, a mark of the course, as I tried to pinch by it. In a racing boat, yes; in a CSY 44, no. We were far enough ahead of the next boat so that rerounding did not lose us second place; only face.

We repeated our second in the second race after a poor first windward leg, when I finally figured out that the lead of the genoa sheet was wrong. I have to admit that this kind of racing had me well tuckered out at the finish, and our evenings were spent quietly aboard *Brunelle*, easing out from the strain. The younger generation did manage some celebrating, and Robert showed up for the last race a bit battered and bruised from an encounter with a ditch. (The circumstances were not fully explained.)

Our big day was the last race, with the same breeze still at a robust 25 to 30 knots. We got a fine, clear start and led the CSY contingent all the way around a course that used Dead Chest, Carrot Rock, Pelican Island, and The Indians as marks—a scenic, windblown tour of some of the special features of the BVI. We were half a mile ahead of Simon, who was in second, at the finish, at the unbelievably early hour of 1310, and it was great to get that one-design thrill of looking back at all your competitors. This first gave us a second in CSY for the series. The prize award ceremony was a relatively decorous affair, and our celebration back on *Brunelle* was a pleasantly low-key one, rubbing sore limbs and muscles. The racing had been fun, and in this one-design mode, no one could bitch about the handicapping.

16

GIRDING LOINS

THE TIME HAD come to gird our loins again for Anegada Passage. What one should gird loins *with* for the Passage, I'm not sure, but that body of water had achieved enough stature in our consciousness to merit being thought of in Biblical terms. With the third leg of CORT scheduled for Antigua, almost 200 miles of sailing to the southeast, we would have to make our way down there in the next two weeks. This meant two overnight passages. Bev had returned to the States, and John and Aimee would be leaving from the BVI, so the team of Robinsons and Jim Lillie, who had helped bring *Brunelle* from the Caicos to the BVI on her voyage down in 1979, would again be the passage crew.

We did clean-up chores at Road Town, like topping off fuel and water and paying bills at CSY and Village Cay, and made Trellis Bay our first stop on the way, a good sail in the still brisk northeaster. Robert, who seemed to have thoroughly enjoyed crewing for us in the regatta despite the encounter with a ditch, insisted on having us as his guests at The Last Resort, and it was a jolly crew's reunion. Under a mop of curly hair he had a round, cheerful face that lit up with pleasure at the slightest provocation, and he was right in his element in the semi-frenetic gaiety of an evening at The Last Resort, bustling around with trays of drinks and bantering with the guests. Tony, for some reason, thoroughly confused us by reversing his by now very familiar (to us) first and second shows. Things were never dull at The Last Resort.

The persistence of the strong northeaster began to assume symbolic status for the passage ahead of us. Anegada was sending us its message that it was out there, waiting for us to test ourselves in its unpredictable pattern of wind and wave. By morning, with the cobwebs from Robert's party gradually defilamenting, it was raining hard, and the wind had freshened even more, but, after a morning of getting phone calls through to the States from the airport public phones, always a lengthy process, I saw the sky begin to brighten. We had a stimulating, satisfying beat, with full sail just manageable in rail-down conditions, to North Sound, taking the shortcut at Mosquito Pass, which I always think of as the back door, as it was getting on in the afternoon by the time we made it.

We tried anchoring off Saba Rock, north of The Bitter End, but the anchored boats were very close together, swinging in wide arcs in the uneven gusts, as the wind funneled in over Saba Rock with extra authority, kicking up quite a chop. Just before dark, I decided to move back to the lee side of Prickly Pear Island, where the water, at least, was flat, but the wind continued its assault, whooshing down the leeward side of Prickly Pear's steep hills with added muscle and unpredictable timing. Despite its moan and whistle in the rigging, we had an easy night at anchor.

I grabbed the opportunity, when boats began to clear out in the morning, to move over to a Bitter End mooring, as the weather continued to deteriorate. Clouds had taken over completely, and the wind was consistently stronger, spitting with rain. It was a constant reminder that Anegada Passage was out there, just beyond Virgin Gorda's last line of defense.

This was very peculiar weather for the time of year. April can be a windy month, but the combination of clouds, wind, and rain persisting day after day was something unusual, in April or any time of year in this area of 95 percent predictable conditions. The five percent was taking more than its share. While Jim, John, and Aimee explored the coves of North Sound by dink, Jane and I read and napped, happy to be on a mooring. To alleviate the danger of cabin fever, we arranged dinner at The Bitter End. We had first eaten here on a bareboat cruise in 1973, when it was just getting started, and we were one of four tables in the dining room for dinner. Now it was practically a production line business, with perhaps 100 visiting yachtsmen joining the hotel guests for dinner each night after radioing ahead for reservations and orders from the menu. This led to an amusing sideshow of overhearing some earnest conversations, such as someone wanting to know "How is the chicken native-style cooked?" One woman, who must have had a racetrack background, asked "What are your entries for tonight?" We learned how the chicken was cooked (with spices), what lobster Bahamian style was, and the various ways grouper was served, practically a cooking course on VHF.

The several sections of the dining room are overwhelmingly nautical in decor, with yacht club burgees by the hundred strung from the overhead, and half models on the walls. With three sides open to the outdoors and a view through palm trees and flowering shrubs across the beach to the boats in the anchorage, it is a highly atmospheric spot, and it has become a traditional highlight of everybody's BVI cruise to have dinner here. That night, the food was good, as usual, but the after-dinner custom of tea or coffee laced with spiced rum out on the terrace was a victim of the weather.

Quite a few boats had gathered in the anchorage as a stepping-off spot for Antigua, and there was a murmur of anxiety, as crews met in the bar, about prospects for the passage, with Anegada naturally topmost in all minds. Moving among them was a sailor I had known for over 20 years, Tom Kelly from Long Island Sound, who had been a shipmate of son Robby in the 1960 Bermuda Race. He was at that time in charge of The Bitter End's sailing program, which features quite a variety of boats for guests' use, from Lasers and Sunfish to Rhodes 19s, J/24s, and now Freedom 30s. When he spied us, he asked me to come to breakfast the next morning with Myron Hokin, the Bitter End's owner. Myron, a Chicago businessman and an enthusiastic cruising sailor, had fallen in love with the Bitter End on a cruising visit in its early days and had decided to buy it. He and his wife, Bernice, are very hands-on owners, spending many weeks there and taking a great interest in every phase of the operation. They had a Texas couple, Janis and Don, as managers, who were accomplished meeters and greeters and administrators, and the place was booming. Bernice's main interest was in the landscaping and gardening, and every inch of the place showed special care and attention. The grounds and the hillsides above are a riot of bougainvillea, hibiscus, and oleander, with flower beds in bloom, and neatly manicured paths along the water leading to the bedroom units in separate cabins.

Myron wanted to pick my brain on what the cruising yachtsman is looking for, as they were really building up the attractions for sailors, and we chatted back and forth for a good time. The latest item on the marine side was a new marina south of the main clubhouse called the Quarterdeck Club. It was to be on a membership basis of $100 a year, but transients would be welcomed for an overnight fee when there were open slips. It could accommodate about 18 to 20 boats, and there were shore power outlets, water hoses, showers, and heads in the small clubhouse building. As a reward, I guess, for my picked brain, I was given a complimentary membership, and as soon as our breakfast meeting was over I moved *Brunelle* into a slip. None too soon—the weather continued to worsen.

Jim, John, and Aimee, undaunted by the conditions, rented Lasers and had a wild time planing (and capsizing) around the anchorage, with one slight mishap of John getting his skull bashed by the boom, with a nasty cut.

The boats hoping to head for Antigua Race Week were waiting out the weather, but one crew of bucko young deck apes, charged with taking a hot racing machine down to Antigua, where their owner would join them, pooh-poohed the words of caution from experienced VI skippers who were not about to head out into Anegada Passage in these conditions. Flexing muscles and beating chests, they had taken off early that morning amid much shaking of heads by the stay-in-ports.

After my crew had given up on Laser sailing, the weather really began to put on a show, and I couldn't have been happier with my new Quarterdeck membership. The wind built until gusts of 50 knots were swooping down on the anchorage. With the conformation of the hills above The Bitter End, wind is always erratic even in normal times, and now it could be called paranoid. A gust would blast in from the north, around Saba Rock, to be followed immediately by a counter blow from the south from the gap at Biras Creek. In between, direct williwaws from the east would shoot straight down from the hilltops. It was a continuous multi-directional onslaught. From our snug berth in the marina, it was quite a show, and it got even more so as now and then there were crazy little tornadoes that would create miniature waterspouts. Whirling and twisting, they would skitter through the anchorage on an erratic course, and helter-skelter rainsqualls burst down and splattered over us.

While all this was going on, the ocean racer that had set out with such bravado a few hours earlier came limping back to the marina, and if she had had a tail, it would have been between her legs. Her oh-so-bucko young men were wide-eyed and gasping in their description of conditions out in the dreaded Passage. One coherent comment I overheard was "The waves were higher than our spreaders!" Sic transit....

The Quarterdeck had the most unusual dockmaster (mistress? person?) I had ever met, a petite, utterly beguiling, dark-haired young woman, half-English, half-Brazilian in a mix of exotic, pixie charm, named Jenny, who was as efficient as she was attractive. She had handled us well on our arrival, and now she was having a busy day as more boats came into the security of the marina.

By nightfall, there was a general inclination to gather and compare notes along the row of slips, and we developed an impromptu cocktail party, with our crew, Tom Kelly, Roland and Lisa from *Klee,* who always seemed to turn up where we were, and Michael Tate, the professional skipper of the Hokins' yacht, a classic character ketch named *Alionora,* which had a permanent berth at Quarterdeck. Michael was a dry, soft-spoken former officer in the British Navy, who had that typical Limey understated, satirical wit. He was a fount of amusing stories, and he told one on himself about the name of his vessel. A feature of her was a figurehead rising imposingly from the stem of a dignified gentleman in regal-looking period regalia, and Michael was often asked about it. He actually had no knowledge of the background of the name or the figurehead, but he cooked up a story to tell people that it was Count Alionora of Bessarabia, who led his people in revolt against the Czar. Almost everyone accepted this, but Michael finally got his comeuppance when a charter guest responded with "I vas born in Bessarabia, and I haf never heard of zis Count Alionora!"

With everyone beginning to chafe with impatience, we had another day of squalls and williwaws, with no improvement whatsoever, a day in which to read and nap and try to be philosophical. We had one small disaster when the main hatch caught a gust and blew over backwards, ripping its fastenings.

Finally, the next morning brought a slight improvement, sun and no rain, but still a blustery wind, which kept alive visions of those spreader-high waves on the other side of the island. (The once-brave ocean racers had not yet tried to go out again.) To be doing something, I took the Bitter End launch to the dock at Gun Creek, a mile away on the south side of the Sound, the nearest road access, and took a taxi to Spanish Town, Virgin Gorda's main settlement, the site of Virgin Gorda Yacht Harbour and the airport. I had cleared out of the BVI in Road Town when I thought John and Aimee would be aboard for the passage to St. Martin. Now that they were leaving I had to turn in a revised crew list to Customs and Immigration at the airport (and I wondered what its runway had been like with 50-knot crosswinds).

The taxi ride up the steep approach road from Gun Creek, past the little native settlement sprawled single-file up the hillside and over the roller-coaster mountain road to town, is always a breathtaking one. Gafford Potter, the contract taxi driver for Bitter End, a typical, shyly smiling, soft-spoken BV islander, has been doing it for years, and he handled the swoops and curves with aplomb.

I did my business, after some confusion at the Immigration office over our change of status, had a cheeseburger at Virgin Gorda Yacht Harbour's Bath and Turtle, bought bananas and cristofine at Buck's, the native market at the marina, and rode back to Gun Creek with Gafford. From the hilltops as the road reached its spectacular crests, I could look out to the limitless seascape to the east and see that the weather was breaking. There were patches of sun glittering on the water, and the clouds were higher and friendlier.

When I started to get out of the taxi at the Gun Creek dock, I realized that I didn't have my grocery package, and I couldn't figure out what I'd done with it. Gafford had no idea when I asked him. Later that night, I got word from the hotel desk that I had a package, and Gafford had delivered it to the launch. I had left it on the counter at Buck's and it was still there when he went back on the chance I might have left it: a nice small-town touch. In the years since, whenever I see Gafford, his face lights in his shy smile, we say "bananas and cristofine," and have a good laugh.

We had more visiting around the marina with Roland and Lisa, and sailing friends from long ago, Pat and Jack Duane, showed up, as sailing friends seem to do in all sorts of places. The rain had almost stopped, the wind was dropping, and we spent a quiet night. By morning it was calm and sunny. John and Aimee left us, as I puttered with temporary repairs to the hatch, and by lunchtime, with pleasantly normal trades blowing and the sun shining brightly, it was obvious that the weather was OK for leaving. Other Antigua-bound boats were pulling out, and we said goodbye to Jenny at 1530. We made sail off Prickly Pear, and headed out for that often thought-of body of water waiting for us between Virgin Gorda and St. Martin.

17

ONWARD

ONCE CLEAR OF all the islands and the sneaky rocks just awash east of Necker Island known as The Invisibles, we found that there was still a fresh northeast trade, and a large bank of clouds was filling in from offshore. It could still be tough out there, another one of those Anegada Passage nights that made our daughter Alice christen it "Oh-my-God-ah" Passage after a particularly rough crossing. There was a lump of sea left over from the "spreader height" conditions, but nothing that bad. Nibbling one of Jane's finger food suppers, we settled down on port tack under reefed main, jib, and staysail, able to hold a rhumbline course of 125°M or a bit higher. Jim and I stood two-hour wheel tricks, with Jane taking 2200–0000 (I reclined in the cockpit on her watch), the same system we had used for night passages on the trip down from the Bahamas. It would not do for an extended voyage, but it worked well for one night.

There were other boats ahead of us on the same course, but they faded from view as darkness fell, leaving us alone in our little cocoon of fiberglass, a world limited by the reflection of the starboard running light on the bow wave and the faint glow of the stern light on the clash of wake astern. We plunged on under the black cloud cover, making good, bouncy progress, and for once Anegada Passage pulled a reverse switch on us. On all our previous crossings, conditions had changed for the worse during the night, but this time the cloud cover started to break up as the moon, just past full, began to make itself known. By the middle of Jane's watch, it was a bright, moonlit night, with the proper glittery path on the water and a visible horizon in all directions. The breeze and wave conditions held through the rest of the night, and with the clear, yellow dawn there was St. Martin, a friendly, encouraging black shape dead ahead.

Of course it would have been too good to imagine that we had been able to hold the rhumbline course right into Great Bay. As the sun took over from the moon in a nice counterpoint on each horizon, the breeze softened and headed us off to 135°, with Saba's dramatic triangle of a peak off the starboard bow. Still, by 0900 we were almost even with St. Martin, some seven miles to the south of it, and we ended up powering into Great Bay through the dozens of anchored boats gently rocking in the surge. Our 1130 arrival was a lot better than our mid-afternoon one last time.

We couldn't raise Bobby's on VHF, and no one appeared on the pier as we drew close, but Jerry Rosen, skipper of the day-tripper sloop *Gabrielle* based there, saw us and waved us in. We had made friends with him on our last visit, leaving him a bunch of books and magazines when we departed. He showed us a berth at the outboard end on the north, or inner side, next to the great white bulk of *Enterprise* gleaming in the sun. Once settled in, it was nap time, then a quiet dinner and early bed, the usual aftermath of Anegada Passage.

Refreshed and ready to get organized, I spent the next morning shopping, with a combined bill of $156 at the food market and commissary. In just the couple of months since our last visit, a case of Mount Gay had gone up to $30. I was short of film for covering Antigua Week and wasted several hours looking for EP 120, my usual type, all over town. I also frittered away half an hour getting a call through to the *Yachting* office in New York—standard procedure here.

One problem that night passage had revealed was that the binnacle light was out, and I spent some time trying to substitute a flashlight for it with no luck. I was referred to Robbie Ferron, who had a boat service operation based at Bobby's, and he took over fiddling with the binnacle. A quiet, friendly South African who reminded us of Peter Clarke, he finally produced a makeshift solution after finding that the fuse was blown at the switch ($10).

Robbie's operation was just beginning at that time, but he built it into a major business over the years, and was a great help to us each time we came to Philipsburg. One summer several years later, we left *Brunelle* in his care for the seasonal layup after a down-island session, instead of taking her all the way back to Tortola, and it worked out very well.

Meanwhile, we had a binnacle light. To tone down its glow, I had to shop for nail polish, something I had never thought of as a marine supply. Another item that didn't seem very nautical but was also needed was a set of coffee cups, and I spent most of the next morning, which was rainy and blowy, shopping around for them in St. Martin's plethora of tourist traps. I guess cruise ship visitors did not often buy coffee mugs, as they were hard to come by, but I finally found some at a place called The Shipwreck Shop. The pattern was horrible, but there was no choice. All the time, I was thinking about getting under way for Antigua.

While I was walking around town, in and out of the shops on the narrow lane of a main street, I gradually became aware that, among the crowds of shoppers, an unusual looking female seemed to be everywhere that I was. Dressed in a red jumpsuit that did well by her figure, she was almost six feet tall, with a head of dark hair and handsome features, and it would be an understatement to say that she was a striking presence. It was impossible not to be aware of the sight of her the first time, and her continued reappearance made her even more noticeable. When I finally settled on the coffee mugs and went back to *Brunelle*, Jane said that a tall girl in a red jumpsuit had been looking for me. I couldn't imagine that there was more than one tall girl in a red jumpsuit wandering around Philipsburg, and in a few minutes, there she was on the pier asking rather timidly if she could speak to me.

I invited her aboard, and, seated in the cockpit, she introduced herself as Mieke Doeff from Holland. She said that she was looking for a ride to Antigua and had been told that we were going there. She admitted, with a shy smile, that she had been following me around town but had not gotten up the nerve to speak to me until now. I have always had a wariness about pier-head jumps and had a basic policy of not taking one on. There had been a case in Samaná, Dominican Republic, on our trip down, when a tearful woman had begged me to take her to Puerto Rico illegally, and I had turned her down, but there was something straightforward and appealing about Mieke (not just the red jumpsuit). She said that Bobby had told her about us, and after a few questions and some more conversation, I agreed to give her a ride. She said she was a moderately experienced sailor and would do whatever chores might be helpful. Jane had taken to her and did not object, so it was settled. She had a duffel parked at the head of the pier, fetched it, and was quickly aboard.

When we had more of a chance to be filled in on her story, it was a sad, interesting, and, unfortunately, typical one, not unusual with the sort of people you meet bouncing around island waterfronts. She and a Dutch boyfriend had taken off from home for a Caribbean adventure, looking to do just that, bouncing around the islands to become involved in come what may. They both had built up savings, Mieke's in Dutch guilders and the young man's in dollars, and they had decided to head for a Dutch area first, using her money and saving his until they got to a dollar area.

It would not be hard to guess what happened. They moved in full blast on the Sint Maarten scene and had a fine time for a while, but Mieke's guilders disappeared fairly quickly and were soon used up. Thereupon, the young man disappeared too, kept his dollars and took off, leaving Mieke flat broke and on her own. What was behind their personal relationship, and why it ended this way, we did not ask.

Fortunately, she had been able to get a job as a stewardess on one of the dude-cruise sailing ships operating out of St. Martin, the *Polynesia*, familiarly known as Polynausea, and she had slaved away in the miserable conditions on board for several months until she had built up some funds again. Now, tired of the drudgery and squalor of a stewardess job, she had quit and was ready for more adventures. She had friends on a boat that was to take part in Antigua Race Week and would have a berth when she got there.

Along with her arrival, the weather began to brighten until, by 1630, it was pleasantly sunny. We had nothing to keep us in St. Martin any longer, and the passage to Antigua would be best as an overnight one so as to arrive in daylight. We checked out, powered out to Pointe Blanche, and made full sail in a pleasant trade of about 12 to 15 knots that allowed us to hold 140°M, which, if it held, would give us a straight shot. It was easy sailing as we slid by St. Barts in the dying light, with Saba standing starkly against the sunset. To cheer us on, the setting sun gave us a green flash, and the moon, in its waning stage, joined us at 2230 to make it a lovely night for sailing. St. Kitts and Nevis were vague shadows to starboard, with an occasional light on shore twinkling through the moonlight glow, and everything would have been perfect if the breeze had not veered southeast a bit, heading us off to 150°. Jane and I split four-on-four-off with Jim and Mieke, and we averaged just under five knots, which is not too bad close-hauled in moderate air.

We found ourselves down to the southwest, near the stark pinnacle of Redonda Island, as a beautiful morning of cheerfully puffy clouds developed. This meant we were almost dead to leeward of Antigua in a diminishing breeze, so the prudent thing was to turn on the power shortly before noon and chug into Deep Bay on Antigua's northwest coast, arriving about 1600. This passage was in contrast to one the previous year, when we left St. Barts at 1900 on a broad reach in a strong northeaster and were off Deep Bay by 0700. Such are the vagaries of this run. The leg down to Antigua is always a roulette wheel, and we had had both kinds of luck, but this was not a strenuous sail by any standard.

We powered our way past the sunken wreck that straddles the entrance to Deep Bay into the nicely secure, beach-girt anchorage inside and dropped the hook in 10 feet off the lovely curve of beach in one of our favorite Caribbean anchorages. Its only drawback is that it is directly under the approach path to Antigua's rather busy jet airport, with the noise that it produces, but it is only at intervals. We spent a calm, pleasant evening, with five other boats scattered around the bay, and Jim soothed us to an early bed with a tape of him playing the flute. Long before our friend the moon peeked over the hills, a deep, heavy sleep was the natural coda to an overnight passage.

18

A SPECIAL ISLAND

ANTIGUA HAD BEEN our introduction to Caribbean sailing back in 1961 (not counting subchaser duty in the Navy), when Jane, Martha, Alice, and I spent eight days out there in the motorsailer *Viking* with the Swedish couple, Brita and Sten Holmdahl (who had given us the idea for hand signals between bow and helm). It was always like old home week to get back, which we had done quite often since then, and Alice had spent a winter there working for the Nicholson family charter office.

The Nicholsons were the pioneers of yacht chartering in the Caribbean, and they have been at the heart of it out of Antigua ever since. Commander Vernon Nicholson, his wife, and their sons Rodney and Desmond, then young teenagers, had set sail from England in 1948 when Vernon retired from the British Navy after World War II, headed, supposedly, for a new life in Australia in the venerable 70-foot, all-teak schooner *Mollihawk*, built in 1903. They put into Antigua after their transatlantic passage and holed up for rest, recreation, and rehabilitation in English Harbour, whose colorful history dated back to its role as a major British naval base in Lord Nelson's day. The harborfront was then an abandoned ruin with the softly tinted red brick walls of its buildings in tumbledown disarray, but the semi-circular stone bulkhead of the naval dockyard was still a fine place to tie up. Before the Nicholsons gathered forces to continue on to the Pacific, they became involved in taking guests out sailing from the Mill Reef Club, Antigua's pioneering luxury resort, and somehow they never did leave.

Mollihawk became the first yacht in their new charter business, and in 1961 she and *Viking* were in a 12-boat fleet of crewed yachts operating under Nicholson management. We had a great cruise in *Viking*, exploring Antigua's southeast coast and then sailing down-island to Martinique. The next

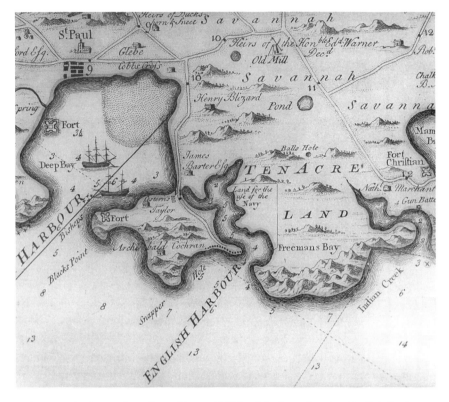

Photograph of a section of an old map (1745) of Antigua showing English Harbour

year we went the rest of the way south, Martinique to Grenada in *Mollihawk*, with a retired British naval officer, John Christian, as skipper, and three islanders as crew. Commander Nicholson had moved ashore, managing things in Antigua, and making daily radio contact with his vessels in a performance that was a highlight of each day's activities. His deep voice, the personification of the British Navy, boomed out across the sea for miles in fatherly concern, advice, and cheerful banter.

This double introduction to Caribbean cruising had started me on a career program of multiple visits and multiple articles and a book or two, and it had been interesting to watch the tremendous development of activity in the years since those first cruises. By now, Rodney and Desmond had taken over the business after Vernon retired, and English Harbour, restored and administered by an organization called Friends of English Harbour, was the booming yachting capital of the Eastern Caribbean, with hundreds of boats

English Harbour, Antigua

based there and activity now expanded to the next bay to the west, Falmouth Harbour. The year before, I had one day counted boats from 26 worldwide ports, ranging from Hong Kong to Aqaba, plus many U.S. harbors, moored stern-to the Dockyard.

Despite this crowding, the place still reeks of atmosphere and a sense of history. Though some walls are still lying in ruins, and old upended cannons are used as bollards, many of the buildings have been restored, occupied now by all the services of a busy marina. I had been there twice before for Race Week and also Dockyard Day, the official dedication of the restoration, amid much pomp and marine pageantry. We had spent a month there the previous winter on our down-island junket, leaving *Brunelle* in the care of a local boatkeeper, Lester Brooks, for $2.00 a day when we came home in March. Lester, who wore beat-up cutoffs and had a very casual manner, was an excellent workman who knew boats in and out and was a walking encyclopedia on famous sailing yachts. After finishing work of an after-noon, he and I would shoot the breeze about boats over a beer.

Antigua is one island that can be cruised for a week or two, with a good choice of harbors, in contrast to most of the Windwards and Leewards, which only have one or two ports, and we had had an interesting time poking into most of its coves and bays. That was how we discovered Deep Bay and why we felt at home there now. It was a perfect spot to unwind after our sail down, but it undergoes a change of personality every morning. From a peaceful, undisturbed hideaway, it suddenly erupts into a beehive of activity between 1000 and 1100 as day-tripper boats from St. John's, the nearby capital city, swarm in and send their passengers ashore to the beach, or diving on the wreck at the entrance. Most noticeable of these is a mammoth tugboat aptly named *Tugboat Annie*, with a big crowd aboard. The atmos-phere undergoes a complete change, as it did this morning.

While all this was taking place, we gradually collected ourselves and got under way, powering the couple of miles around the point into St. John's to enter Customs and Immigration. I wanted to get this over with before going to English Harbour, which is also a port of entry, and has a fair claim to being the rubber stamp capital of the Caribbean. There is a designated quarantine anchorage in Freeman Bay outside English Harbour's inner bay, where incoming boats have to anchor, put up the O flag, and await the pleasure of the Customs and Immigration officers. Usually they are far from in a hurry in getting to the waiting boats, and it can sometimes take up to half a day, along with a very officious session of stamp banging, when they finally get around to you. There had been one sergeant in charge of the operation in years past who was so officious and arbitrary that, in response to hundreds of complaints from the yachting fraternity, he was finally removed from office. Now things had improved a bit as to the civility of the reception, but it was still a slow process, and I decided to avoid it by going into St. John's.

The office at St. John's is at the ship terminal and is mainly for the cruise ships that are big business for Antigua. Very few yachts use it, but we have, now and then. The problem is that there is no landing place for sailboats, as the side of the pier is of cruise ship proportions. But there is a solution: The tugboats that work the cruise ships tie up to the pier between jobs, and they can be used as a "stepping stone."

The harbor is a deep indentation of almost two miles between the low brown hills of Antigua's northern half on the starboard and a complex of oil tanks, service areas, and the ship terminal to port. The grubby city itself is

English Harbour, Antigua

at the inner end. St. John's has little to recommend it, except for its complete protection and the convenience of a major supermarket at the waterfront, with a better stock and lower prices than at English Harbour. The city of 25,000 is hot and dirty, with no architectural distinction, and a horrendous near-gridlock of traffic in its narrow streets.

If there had been a cruise ship at the terminal, we would not have gone in, but this was a ship-less day, and we got permission to tie up to a tugboat so I could scramble up on it and then get ashore from its high foredeck. It was suffocatingly hot alongside the steel of the tug's hull, from which the sun's glare reflected fiercely, so I tried to make quick work of the visit. The young clerk in the office, far down a long corridor in the airless interior of the pier shed, was polite and cordial, not always the case with Antiguan

English Harbour, Antigua

officials. He was, though, exquisitely slow and precise in his handling of the paperwork and the inevitable thumping of rubber stamps, but I finally got our cruising permit, good for a month, and our clearance. The berth at the tug had cost us the traditional donation of a few paperbacks and magazines, which we were glad to do. We then made a quick shopping expedition, dinghying into the supermarket from a close-in anchoring spot. For some reason they would not take American Express travelers checks, but I fortunately had enough cash, and we were happy to escape the stifling atmosphere at 1500 to power on outside and make sail.

The leeward side of Antigua has better sailing than under most of the other, higher islands, as the trades come unimpeded across the low hills, compared to the fickle calms and backwinds of such mountainous islands as Guadeloupe, Dominica and Martinique. We had a fast reach in smooth water past Deep Bay and Five Islands Bay to Johnson Island, the little cay off the southwest tip of Antigua. Then, since it was getting late, we powered

Nelson's Old Naval Shipyard

to windward the seven miles to Falmouth Harbour, inside Cade's Reef and along the south shore, dropping the hook at 1820 as twilight dimmed.

Falmouth was crowded but peaceful, with a cool breeze off the shore. It is five miles by water around the next headland and into English Harbour, but English Harbour is only a five-minute walk from the informal little Antigua Yacht Club and its dinghy dock at the northeast corner of the bay, and Mieke and I went over after dinner. She found the friends she was joining on a Swan 38, and I elbowed and shouldered my way into the body crush at the bar at the Admiral's Inn.

This lovingly restored building, once an officers' mess in Nelson's day, is the keystone of English Harbour's restored atmosphere, with its brick walls, dark, heavy beams across the white of the low ceiling, period furniture, and a graceful, palm-girt terrace outside, looking over the harbor. A large painting of Horatio scowls down over the scene from behind the bar. As imperturbable as he was reputed to be, even Nelson would undoubtedly have been taken aback by the scene there on this Saturday night before the start of the Race Week. The sailing crowd was ass-to-ass and shoulder-to-shoulder in every inch of the place, and it was so crowded that the perpetual darts game outside the door to the men's room had to be suspended.

This was the usual CORT cacophony as experienced at the Rolex and BVI, with an added touch of atmosphere in these surroundings, perhaps a higher concentration of sweat and noise under the low ceiling, and back slapping reunions the order of the occasion. There were well-known sailors from many points, and I bumped into people like Halsey Herreshoff, Roz and Barry Rice, and many more old friends. As the evening and the Mount Gays wore on, I developed an impression that the place was full of identical clones, all with beards. Another race week in the Caribbean was about to begin.

19

A GROWING TRADITION

THIS WOULD BE the 14th Antigua Race Week, thoroughly established as a major feature of the yacht racing calendar, with 104 entries, and a far cry from the regatta's beginnings. The Nicholsons had conceived it originally as a jolly picnic for the charter fleet when the busy season ended in May, and it consisted of one race and a barbecue, with no one very worried about how they did in the racing, and some ancient character vessels out there for laughs. This attitude did not last long, however, as most sailors have an inborn compulsion to sail faster than the boats near them. In a couple of years, the schedule was expanded to several races, and it was obvious that almost everyone was getting serious about the racing.

My introduction to it was at the fourth edition in 1971. There was still an aura of picnic-type fun about it, but the racing had become completely serious. There were five days of it, and the fleet consisted of 25 boats, with an ocean-racing class of 16 split into two divisions at 35 feet LOA, a cruising class, and a "classic" class. In addition to the yacht racing, there were such special events as motorboat rallies, workboat races, a Sunfish regatta, and a spearfishing contest.

The handicapping was done via that West Indies Rule, which was still in use in 1981 at all CORT regattas. It had been considerably modified, pulled apart, and put back together again over the years. (The rumor spread by many racing sailors that it had been concocted over a brew of Babincourt rum and magic mountain herbs by an obeah witch in Haiti was really not true.) Dedicated yachtsmen had worked hard on it, and it was a pretty fair rule as long as nobody went to the expense of building to beat it, and nobody had.

Enzian, the author's first Antigua Race Week berth

In 1977 I had been asked to be the official regatta photographer, and it was amazing what development there had been in six years. The entry was over 60 boats from 17 countries, with some of the sport's top competitors there to enjoy the combination of serious, hotly contested action in a glamorous setting, enhanced by some of the best parties anywhere on the world's racing circuits. Now, of course, the 104 boats in 1981 were proof of its continued attraction, and by the 1990s the list had grown to more than 200 boats.

Those 1971 and 1977 regattas were two of the best assignments I had ever booked for myself (there are certain privileges to being Editor), and they rated among the most memorable fun ever. In 1971 I was a crewmember aboard the defending champion from 1970, *Enzian*, a Westphal 38, owned by a Puerto Rican obstetrician, Dr. Cesar Berries, who was a good sailor and a delightful skipper. In the crew were Howard Hulford and Ed Shearin, managing partners at Curtain Bluff Hotel, and a couple of native hands. Howard, a former commercial airplane pilot, who had a bald head and an Otto von Bismarck handlebar moustache and the put-on manner of a Prussian colonel (that was all an act) had been a co-founder of the regatta with Desmond Nicholson, and was the kind of guy who got things done. Curtain Bluff, where Jane and I stayed, was one of the best-run resort hotels I have ever known, and Howard's supposedly stern manner as a manager was belied by a very real involvement in the welfare of the nearby native village that supplied the staff, with such activities as tennis instruction and court privileges for the local youths. It was a special crew to be a part of, and we had a great time in the racing.

Strangely enough, Antigua did not live up to its reputation for good sailing conditions that 1971 week, as they were mostly light and fluky. This hurt *Enzian*, as she was a heavy boat, and a decision had been made to measure her with a 150 percent genoa, instead of 180, expecting the usual heavy breezes. Conditions were so light on the race from Dickinson Bay to Curtain Bluff in a fading sou'wester, something absolutely unheard of here, that only six boats made the finish-line committee's 1800 deadline. We were only 200 yards away and still making some progress when the door was shut, and most of the fleet, including us, was listed as "retired," cutting them out of any chance in the overall standings. Of course, this cut us out of any chance of defending the championship, even though we did well in the other races, winning the first in the only strong breeze. This experience had an important influence on my complaint about the same procedure at the Rolex.

It was all such a good experience, though, that the fun was not spoiled, and the accompanying bacchanalia made up for any disappointment. The parties varied from beach picnics at Curtain Bluff and Dickinson Bay to the jammed-in scene at the Admiral's Inn bar, and the finale of a formal, prize-awards ball beneath the floodlit palms on the Inn's terrace, with everybody on best behavior, at least at the start of the evening. Behind them all were the liquid rhythms and thumping beat of steel bands, while sailors, shoved in together, made the usual hand gestures, elbows akimbo, illustrating "we were on starboard tack, see, and—" and the beer and rum added their distinctive tang to the atmosphere.

The events like the workboat race and the Sunfish regatta produced a lot of laughs and excitement. The workboats, rugged native-built auxiliary sailboats, under-rigged, heavy, and with big cabins, were allowed a certain amount of fuel that had to be judiciously rationed to get them around the course in the best way, and it was quite a sight to see these stalwart craft roaring along in clouds of exhaust as part of their act.

The "classic" fleet was an unusual one: a home-made 19-foot junk that had sailed singlehanded from Europe, a 100-foot schooner, and a tiny 16-foot cabin sloop, *Psammead*, with a rig smaller than a Snipe and a spinnaker the size of the skipper's hat. She was the only one of the trio to finish all the races, winning for her skipper, who happened to be a Methodist missionary, the prize of a case of scotch.

I had one personal experience that was memorable in its own way. The pressure change of the jet flight down had managed to stir up a tooth, and it produced a consistent ache that would not subside. I took a lot of aspirin to no avail, and Howard and Ed gradually became aware of my problem. With lay-day approaching, I thought I should possibly see a dentist, and I asked about the situation in Antigua.

"Oh yeah," was the answer. "He's Chinese—Dr. Fong."

"Is he any good?" I asked.

"Well, his motto is 'Dr. Fong pull your fang.'"

I flinched at this, and the skipper happened to overhear us.

"Having trouble, Bill?"

I described the problem and explained that aspirin had not worked. He pondered for a moment and then said "Well, maybe I have something that will help."

"Anything, anything!" was my reply amid visions of Dr. Fong grappling my fang with chopsticks or something, and Cesar came up with a large white pill. I took it eagerly, and it worked. In a short while the pain was gone, and continued doses kept it that way.

Cesar finally admitted, "I thought it might work. It's a pill I give women when they're having severe labor pains."

I didn't have a baby and was comfortable for the rest of the week.

Things had become much more "big time" by 1977, when I was made a member of the committee. A T-shirt emblazoned with "Antigua Week Race Committee" in large, scarlet letters proved it, and I loved to show it off in other places afterwards. I had never been an official photographer before, and it meant a fascinating mélange of methods for covering the racing, from airplane flights to rides in fast powerboats and a berth in the ex-America's cup 12-Meter *Heritage*, now owned by the head of the Vic Tanney fitness program.

We were again happily billeted at Curtain Bluff in a wonderful suite called the "penthouse" at the top of the hill crowning the outer end of the

Lay-Day Action, Antigua Race Week

point that Curtain Bluff covers. There was a magnificent view 40 miles south across the tradewind-swept seas to the purple shadow of Guadeloupe, and nearby vistas of the windward and leeward beaches of the point, the tennis courts, and the hotel's low buildings scattered amid the lush plantings of trees and gardens. We could have happily spent the week there enjoying the view and wandering down to the beach for a swim, as Jane did for much of the time, while I went about my responsibilities. It was a much better week for pictures than in 1971, as the tradewinds were at their best behavior in the 20- to 25-knot range, and the action was continuous and colorful.

My camera was a Mamiyaflex, a twin-lens Japanese version of a Rollei, with the added feature of a wide angle and telephoto lenses, and I was quite fond of it. It had replaced the original Autocord that was my introduction to any photography more complicated than a Brownie. As an editor, I much preferred working with the 2 1/4″ × 2 1/4″ format of 120 film for its clarity and flexibility for cropping, which is why I had stuck with it. It did have a drawback in that there are only 12 shots on a 120 roll, and you sometimes have to change film just when the action gets good, in contrast to the 35mm. users, who can keep clicking away like mad.

My first day behind the lens was to be in an airplane, and I was driven up island to the airport by a young woman of the committee. I met the pilot, a raffish ex-RAF type, and was about to get aboard when the committee person brought up a man with several cameras hanging around his neck and asked me if I minded if another photographer came along. It was a four-seater plane, and, as a newcomer on the job trying to be cooperative, I said sure. He was a stocky Frenchman with a broad, pock-marked face and a wild head of hair, and he seemed properly grateful as we tucked ourselves into our seats.

It was another matter, though, when we slanted down over the boats off English Harbour. As soon as we circled into shooting position, no matter whether I was at my window and ready to operate, he would lean across me roughly, shoving past me and taking up the whole window, clicking away like mad with one of his 35mms. The fact that he had not showered recently didn't make this act any more attractive.

Our communication through the noise of the engine and language diffi-culties was not the smoothest, but, after a couple more of his push and shove intrusions, I got through to him, mostly via gestures, that he was to stay on his side of the cabin, which he did with very poor grace.

Still, it was a great way to take in the spectacle of the race, and the patterns the boats made, as well as the play of colors over the different water depths, were photographically challenging. We soared high, then swooped low and banked sharply around, and it was one time when I regretted the slow pace of 12-exposure 120. Banging away on a 35mm. as my "colleague" was doing when the action was on his side, would have produced more results. I was sure, though, that I had enough aerial stuff by the time the pilot took us back over the southern hills of Antigua and across the central lowlands, baked brown under the sun, to the airport. My stowaway friend left without a word of thanks when we landed, and we studiously ignored each other when we crossed paths at parties later on. I'm sure I could guess what kind of anchoring habits he would have on a sailboat (but of course some of my best friends are French, *bien entendu*).

It wasn't until I finished the aerial phase of my duties that Howard Hulford casually informed me that I was lucky. The previous year, the photo plane had crashed in the water, but "it wasn't so bad." The photographer, a local female, only had a broken collarbone and lost her equipment. Could have been a lot worse, eh?

The powerboat coverage was an exercise in keeping my equipment dry as we bounced our way around the fleet in a big Boston Whaler, but there was plenty of action, especially at buoy roundings, and the spinnaker colors flashing under the tropical sun over a tropical sea are almost foolproof camera material. The two days in the powerboat produced much the best results, and a particular one was of *Pen Duick VI* in a total spinnaker screw-up, with a man airborne by the halyard and the great sail streaming free from the masthead. It was just too bad that I didn't have sound effects too, to record the screaming *tohu-bohu* on deck. She was the 72-foot ketch owned by the famous singlehanding long voyager Eric Tabarly. He sometimes sailed her alone, but now had a howling horde of his French compatriots as a racing crew.

When I reported aboard *Heritage* at the Dockyard early in the morning of my race day in her, her crew was obviously larger than the normal 11-man racing complement of a 12-Meter. The deck apes were imported Vic Tanney instructors, bulging with muscles, and the midships looked like a Chicago Bears training session. The men were allowed to bring dates, and, along with the afterguard and supernumeraries like me, the souls aboard numbered 21. It was a jolly mob scene, and I was stationed on the fantail as the best place to be out of the way and have freedom to take pictures. I had sailed in the 12-Meters *Weatherly*, *American Eagle* and *Constellation* in training and photo workouts, but this would be my first race in one.

One of the requirements for the dates who came along was that they had to go topless, and there did not seem to be any reluctance about this. Mostly, they perched decorously on the rail around the cockpit or where weight counted on the windward deck. It made a small problem for taking deck action shots for a non-*Playboy* type family-oriented magazine, but I shot away anyway, and one picture that I used in the photo spread in *Yachting* showed a topless girl, actually the female professional aboard who was an involved member of the racing team, working a winch. Conveniently for our purposes, the binnacle was blocking out her upper torso. I have sailed fairly often with a topless wife, so it was not completely strange, and it was interesting how quickly everyone became matter-of-fact about it.

My method as official photographer was to shoot one roll for the committee and one for myself, marking them as I finished them, so they got most of the ones with topless exposure. What they did with them, I don't know.

There were one or two odd little moments. I was spreading Sea-and-Ski sunburn cream on myself, and one of the girls came and asked me if she could have some. Her only pale skin was where the bra was not, and I had a momentary flash of a dirty old man's lustful fantasy that she might want me to apply it (a ridiculous idea, of course). I handed her the tube, and she proceeded to put the stuff on her ankles.

The other incident came when one of the visiting dates, who had never been on a sailboat before, had to go to the head. The female professional was below at the moment, and the visitor came down to her and demurely whispered, "Where is the washroom?" Going topless had not bothered her a bit, but she let out a shriek of dismay when the girl pro lifted a grid in the cabin sole and pointed to the toilet sitting there in a shallow well, wide open for all to see.

Despite the mob scene on deck, the racing was serious (and *Heritage* eventually won the racing division). There is a wonderful sense of urgency and drama when a 12-Meter is charging along rail down in a good breeze. When there was tacking, the sails flapped thunderously, the sheets flailed, the grinders whirred in a frantic scream, and the Vic Tanney muscles rippled and bulged. Fortunately, no topless female fell overboard.

Roaring along on a reach, with *Pen Duick*, our main threat, alongside, we approached a turning buoy, scattering smaller boats that had started earlier out of our way like a fox among chickens, and we had a clear inside overlap on *Pen Duick*. Tabarly was a master seaman all by himself 1000 miles offshore, but he was in a different world in the close-in maneuvering of a race. I knew the story that he had tried out as skipper of a French America's Cup challenger and had revealed complete ignorance of racing rules and the finer points of steering in split-second action, but here he was, standing at the rail and waving us away with circular arm motions, crying "NO RHOOM! NO RHOOM!" All the response he got from our skipper was a single, stiff upthrust arm motion as we continued into the mark with right-of-way, jibed in a great crash and thrash of action, and sped on to victory well ahead of the frustrated French. (It's only coincidence that all the bad guys have been French. Honestly.)

That was the high point of a memorable week, and being in Antigua again brought back the memories. We would not be billeted in a luxury suite at Curtain Bluff this time, just our convertible bunk in *Brunelle*, and I would not be scrambling around the steeply tilted deck of a 12-Meter amid topless females. We would just be spectating and photographing from our boat, but it was good to be back.

20

FUN AND GAMES

THERE WAS AN early stirring of activity, as the race boats basing in Falmouth headed out into a bright breezy day for an 0900 start the next morning. Somehow, after the crack-of-dawn beginnings to my official days in '77, it was a pleasant contrast to relax over breakfast in the cockpit and see the transoms of the racing boats disappear around the point. The course that day was all in waters outside English Harbour, and I would catch up with them later.

With morning chores complete, I rowed to the Yacht Club dinghy dock and walked to the Dockyard to check with the committee. There were 28 boats that had sailed in the first two CORT regattas, and I wanted to get their standings to date, as my *Yachting* story would be on the complete CORT circuit. I checked at the information desk at committee headquarters and asked the woman on duty if they had a copy of the CORT standings for the press.

"Cort? What is cort?" was her response in that snippy, upwardly inflected tone the British use in handling an annoying question. Despite her official position, she seemed to have never heard of CORT, and, as the week went on, I found that this was not unusual among Antiguans. They had not sent any local boats to the two VI regattas, so the 28 contenders for the series title were all visitors, who had bashed their way the 200 miles to windward down there in the miserable spell of weather we had been having. As far as the pale, drawn-featured Limey lass knew, I could have been asking for the Ivy League lacrosse standings, and she acted as though I was some sort of public nuisance. Local navel watching seemed to be a prominent Antiguan attitude.

Casting about for somebody more helpful, I ran into Desmond Nicholson's wife Lisa at the Admiral's Inn. A tall, willowy, dark-haired American of noteworthy charm, she greeted me with enthusiasm based on acquaintance going back to our first visit in 1961 and asked if I would like a ride up to Shirley Heights to get a look at the racers. This was just what I'd been hoping for, and it would be a good photo opportunity, so I accepted happily.

Shirley Heights is on the east side of English Harbour, rising to almost 1000 feet. In colonial days, when the fleet was based here, the hilltop was fortified, and it controlled the harbor entrance. Now it is a popular sightseeing spot, with a steeply winding road up to a parking area. There is a magnificent view over Freeman Bay, the Dockyard, and the whole south coast of Antigua, with Guadeloupe looming on the horizon. That morning, in sparkling sunshine and the breeze fresh in our faces, the panoramic view under our feet, as it were, filled with over 100 sailboats spread over the blue of the sea, was a breathtaking one. Some were beating eastward to a buoy off Willoughby Bay, and others were on the run back to Curtain Bluff under spinnaker. There are few sights to match this in the world of yacht racing, and a crowd of spectators was there to enjoy it. Far off, beyond the Dockyard, part of Falmouth was visible, including one small dot that was *Brunelle*, and I got a private kick out of the fact that she was a tiny part of this spectacular scene.

Lisa delivered me back down the hill, and I spent the afternoon dinghy-visiting boats in Falmouth as they came in from the race. One was *Troon*, which had once been on the cover of *Yachting*. She was now owned by a Venezuelan who had met me when we were sailing there several years before. He invited me aboard for a drink of their special rum, Cacique, which could hold its own with Mount Gay and the best Babincourt. Actually, Antigua has its own local rum, Cavalier, which is also quite a good one, and it was the drink of choice much of this week. I found it was a bit *de trop* to ask for Mount Gay in Antigua. Later, Roz Rice dinghied over to invite us to dinner on *Gypsy Dane*, and we had another pleasant visit with them.

The next morning, I did chores and took the laundry to one of the ubiquitous native women who hang around the Dockyard. They do laundry and cleaning, and some of them set up a small stand of fruit and vegetables. Aside from their direct costs, the price of business with them is always a donation to their church, and their operations are a reminder of the contrast between the display of wealth and luxury in the yachts and the native standard of living. Of course, without the yachts and tourists, Antigua would have no economic base, as farming and sugar plantations have long since vanished under the surge of tourism. I found Mrs. Baltimore, a rotund, dignified lady with a deep voice and fleeting smile, who had done our laundry the year before, forgetting, for the moment, until I got the bundle back that afternoon for $22 E.C. (Eastern Caribbean, about 40 cents on the U.S. Dollar) that she was the Clorox queen of the Caribbean. When I picked it up, there was an overpowering olfactory reminder.

In the afternoon, I went out to the point that encloses the Dockyard and Freeman Bay to watch the boats finishing off the entrance. It was now a glossy, modern fleet on the whole, and character vessels had all but disappeared. The 12-Meter star this time was Warren Brown's *War Baby* from Bermuda, the former *American Eagle* in which Robby had been a grinder with John Nichols as crew boss in 1964, and I got a kick out of seeing her again. There was one very unusual boat, an 80-foot gaff schooner sailed by a crew of just two, a man and a woman, who seemed to be able to handle her beautifully. I stayed away from the shambles on shore for a quiet evening with friends on *Brunelle*.

Tuesday, which started in heavy rain but obligingly cleared up by mid-morning, was lay-day, a bit of terminology that always causes giggles and titters among the ladies, and we dressed ship in honor of the occasion, the only time our signal flags had been used in quite some time. Lay-day is planned for fun and games in the area of Antigua Yacht Club for the young crewmembers. There are events like oarless paddling races in rubber dinghies, a tug of war, Sunfish races, continuous steel band music, a beach picnic, and that most chauvinistic of all activities, a wet T-shirt contest (for the girls, naturally). The beer consumption was high and continuous, and the energy expended phenomenal, as we older types sat on the sidelines and tried to remember what it was like when we were young and foolish.

As a dignified counterpoint, the Desmond Nicholsons had a cocktail party at their hilltop house, a beautiful perch with a wide view of the now somewhat degenerated goings-on down below. It was a congenial gathering of friends from Antigua, the Virgins, the States, and points beyond, and I was glad that some of the guests commented that *Brunelle*'s dress-ship added a good touch to the scene. Mieke was there and said she had been having a fine time. (She had not gone in the wet T-shirt contest, but I think she might very well have won!) As for Jim Lillie, he had had crew berths and had mixed into all the festivities, and we had seen very little of him.

Curtain Bluff, Antigua

The scene shifted to the north end of the island for the next couple of days, and we had a good sail following the fleet up there. Activity was at Dickinson Bay off the northwest coast, where triangular courses were used and the trades blew fresher than ever. The action was good and close as the various class leaders began to emerge, and I wondered who the official photographer was this time, as the opportunities were endless for good shots (and I had not heard of any plane crashes). I got all I needed for *Yachting*'s coverage very quickly.

The evening beach picnic at Dickinson Bay had an unusual atmosphere. The whole length of broad, white beach along the shore, perhaps half a mile, backed by bluffs with hotels sprawled across them, was strung with food stands and driftwood fires, operated by locals, and the mobs of celebrating sailors wandered along, stopping for a beer here and a hot dog there, with the pinpricks of firelight throwing shadows against the palms and across the sand in flickering patterns. There was a big crowd, but the way it was spread along the beach in the rather eerie darkness made for a much different ambience from the shoulder-to-shoulder gang fights in places like the Admiral's Inn bar or the even more confined rooms of the little Yacht Club. It was an unusual crowd scene.

The week had one sad and shocking incident. A well-known sailor from the West Coast, Don Vaughan, a former pro football player in his 40s, who was a fixture at major sailing events all over the world, dropped dead of a heart attack during the third race, while hauling on the spinnaker halyard on a Swan 65 named *Mehitabel*. A huge, muscular guy, friendly and cheerful and everyone's favorite shipmate, who used his football player's strength on the toughest jobs on a boat, he had dropped to the deck like a stone, without warning. A radio call was put out for any doctor on a nearby boat, and one was aboard very quickly, but it was already too late.

For his many good friends, this put quite a damper on the week, but the action went on for the bulk of the assemblage, winding up with colorful ceremonies back at English Harbour. We had a fine, brisk sail down there ahead of the fleet, which was sailing a longer course around buoys. We thought of stopping at Curtain Bluff, but it looked surgy, and we continued on to Falmouth. A sad sight there was *Troon*, sitting dismasted at a pier off an apartment house complex, one of the multiple dismastings in that year's CORT. I saw my Venezuelan friend on shore later, and he was very unhappy at this fate. That evening was another version of the Admiral's Inn madhouse, where the fraternizing was frantic, and, as the evening wore on, I seemed to find more and more old fraternizing friends. I did not get back aboard until after midnight, and I just might have been arrested for RWI (Rowing While etc. etc.)

It was a rainy, blowy night, with the boats swinging erratically at anchor, and the rain held on into the morning, when I went to the Dockyard trying to get the final results. The ladies at the information desk were setting new standards of inefficiency and lack of cooperation, but I did get the CORT standings from Louise Johnson, wife of the skipper of *Blue Bayou*, which had ended third in CORT. The winner was the defending champion, John Foster's J/24 *Antidote* from St. Thomas, which had been virtually unbeatable throughout, and which he had wisely shipped to Antigua on a cruise ship, avoiding the 200-mile windward thrash, a rough go in a light boat that size. *War Baby* had not figured in CORT but had matched *Heritage*'s record by taking the racing division here.

The fact that no Antiguan boats had taken part in the CORT series and few Antiguans had paid any attention to it, was an indication that it was not on a sound basis, and Antigua's connection did not last long. It dropped out a year after a Puerto Rican regatta was added, making it a CORC (Conference) instead of a CORT (Triangle). CORT now consists of the three northern regattas, and Antigua Race Week is independent.

Green Island, Antigua

It was like a Who's Who of racing sailors, with everyone milling around the Dockyard. I had one of those unexpected reunions sailors have in all parts of the world, which means that they are not really so unexpected after all, when I ran into George Legakis, an active, dedicated Greek yachtsman with whom we had visited in Athens and sailed in the Aegean, and who had cruised with us in *Brunelle* in the BVI the year before. He and his American friend, Betsy Shaw, who had also sailed with us that time, had been on a Greek cruise ship in the Caribbean and had stopped by Antigua afterwards to check on the sailing action.

We had a good reunion over lunch on *Brunelle*, remembering shared laughs with George. When we had named *Tanagra*, our Out Island 36, for a Greek figurine of a lady dressed to go traveling, dating from the fourth century B.C., I told George, "Hey! We've given our new boat a Greek name. It's TANagra."

I thought I had the pronunciation right, but I can never come up with the right way to say Greek words, and George let me know it.

"No, no," he said. "Ees not TANagra. Ees TaNAGra."

Properly chastised, we pronounced it that way thereafter.

A year later, I got George a berth in the Newport–Bermuda Race, and it was a rough one. When I ran into him in Bermuda after the race, I asked him how it was.

"Oh, it was ROUGH," he moaned. "It was so wet and rough the water was coming in the boat like NiaGARA!"

So I hooted and said, "Look who tries to teach me pronunciation!"

After our luncheon laughter, we had a sightseeing ride around Antigua's byways. In the evening, final ceremonies for the week included a colorful exhibition in which the Antigua Police Band in their starched white jackets, black pants, and London Bobby helmets, sounded Retreat, with precision marching and stirring music in the eerily lit, dramatic setting of the Dockyard. Jane and I passed up the prize awards affair to have dinner with George and Betsy at the Catamaran Club, a native-run restaurant on the beach at Falmouth that had very good food (lobster and wahoo) and a most attractive atmosphere on a waterfront terrace under the palms.

As a final reminder of Antiguan whoop-de-do, a disco on a pier next to Antigua Yacht Club (since silenced by decree) blared out its thumping wails and screeches until 0445. Sleep was hard to come by.

I was finally able to wheedle a makeshift result sheet out of the information desk ladies the next morning, spent my last E.C. cash on bananas and tomatoes (and a church donation) with one of Mrs. Baltimore's friends, cleared out with the officials, and collected Mieke for her return to St. Martin with us.

I also again broke my rule against pier-head jumps and was persuaded by a friend (now I'm not sure he was one) to give one of his crew a ride back to the BVI. This time, as it usually is, it was a mistake. He was wiry and dark, with a scruff of beard, in his 20s. His name was Steve, and in his first few hours aboard he managed to alienate us pretty thoroughly with a wise-ass, know-it-all manner, and a lack of even the bare basics of good manners, ashore or as a guest afloat. He knew nothing about cruising boats, but "knew-it-all" about everything. When we got under way at 1150 and sailed up the coast to Deep Bay, he told us that everything was wrong with our rig (we should have had all the features of an IOR racer), and he tried to devise a makeshift vang "to make the main set better." This was not a generational thing, as Jim Lillie soon took a strong dislike to him, but Mieke seemed to tolerate him, evidently not yet having learned her lesson about young men.

So it was not a happy ship that bid farewell to the fun and games of Antigua Race Week.

21

DISSENSION IN THE RANKS

A LAST SAIL, at least for this year, along the now very familiar west coast of Antigua, brought many memories, and I enjoyed the easy slide in smooth water as landmarks slipped by, trying to ignore my pestiferous new crewman. He was never going to make *Brunelle* into an IOR racer, and I told him so, diplomatically, I thought, hoping to give him the benefit of the doubt and trying to be friendly on his first day aboard, but to no avail. When he settled in sulky silence on the windward rail under the shadow of the main, I did my best to ignore him and take in the scenery to starboard, storing the images mentally for the northern months to come. We bade a silent farewell to Curtain Bluff and its many good memories as its beaches gleamed in the sun, and our guest "penthouse" room stood out atop the end of the point.

Rounding Johnson Island and heading up the coast, we had the beautiful wide beaches of the southwest coast as a bright border between blue sea and green trees, and the Five Islands loomed up ahead. These little rocky cays string off to the west from the main island, marking the entrance to the fine, usually deserted harbor inside, and I had developed enough confidence through frequent sails to take the cut between them instead of detouring offshore around the outer one. It is a narrow passage, with surge breaking over rocks close aboard on each hand, and guests have been known to look at me with questioning doubt when I keep heading for the slot, but there is plenty of water and just enough room. Then Hawksbill Reef must be avoided just north of the Five Islands, but there is usually a small breaking of surge over it to reveal it, which there was this time. Inshore, on another lovely spread of beach, standing on a bluff, Hawksbill resort, where we spent the night on our first Antiguan visit in 1961, looked trim and inviting as the afternoon sun slanted into it.

From there it is a short leg into our old friend, Deep Bay, where I planned to gather forces for a while before taking off on an overnight run to St. Barts. The day-trippers had left, and only a couple of small local sloops and one anchored ketch remained, as we threaded our way by the very visible obstacle of the mid-harbor wreck and found a good spot to anchor not far off the beach in 10 feet over white sand. That same afternoon light, lower now, spread a soft glow over the water and the beach and turned the brown hills around the harbor to gold. It was a peaceful haven.

The younger generation immediately went snorkeling on the wreck and reported it excellent, while I took a short nap to make up for the disco interruptions of the night before, and to prepare for the watchstanding ahead. Jane had a supper of tuna casserole and cole slaw ready as the sun disappeared in a crimson curtain, and by 2000 we were all set to leave. It was a dark evening of no moon and gathering clouds as we cleared by little Sandy Island off St. John's at 2100 in a very light southeast trade. Now that it was May, the trades generally tended more in the southeast, and we sailed under main and wung-out staysail, lazing along over a moderate bobble of sea. Steve, Jim, and I stood two-hour wheel tricks, and the night passed easily (I even managed some sleep) until the clouds, thickening as the hours wore on, began to produce rainsqualls. They did not affect wind direction or strength, just got us wet. By 0700 we had made 40 miles in 10 hours, not exactly record-breaking, and the rain continued until about 0900, when St. Barts appeared dimly over the bow. It had been so dark and cloudy during the night that Nevis and St. Kitts had not made themselves known. The rain came back, so that St. Barts was playing hide-and-seek with us, until we finally powered in on our refrigerator hour and took up the standard fore-and-aft anchoring position at 1400 in a tight fit between the usual mob of boats in Gustavia. This anchoring method in Gustavia was the only time we ever used our spare anchor, a Danforth, as the stern one.

There was visiting ashore by Jim, Steve, and Mieke while Jane and I unwound over cockpit cocktails, and a good old "hashandpeas—etc." sent us to an early bed, absolutely routine after a night passage.

The next day was our own version of lay-day. Steve and Mieke took off to explore, and, using the phone at Loulou's, obligingly made available, I got in touch with my cousin, Ira Wheeler, and his wife Mary, who were staying in a house on shore, to arrange for them to spend a day aboard with us. Jim remained with us, and we powered out to Baie Colombier in almost flat calm for a session at anchor of swimming and beachcombing. It was remarkable how relaxing it was not to have Steve around, and a prime example of how one misfit can disrupt a crew. We had a quietly pleasant day, with the place almost completely to ourselves.

Back in Gustavia, Ira and Mary took us on a tour of St. Barts' steep roads in their rental Mini-Moke, and Ira invited us to dinner at a recommended restaurant named Chez François. As we were having a cocktail, we overheard people at the next table being told that there was nothing on the menu but bacon and eggs, as there was some problem in the kitchen. We quietly paid for the drinks and slipped out to another spot the Wheelers had heard of, Village St. Jean, where we had a decent meal of coquilles St. Jacques.

Mieke, who reported that she had had a pleasant enough day with Steve at the Beach, said she wanted to cook us a thank-you dinner to "pay for her passage." I knew her funds were minimal, but she insisted, and I dinghied her to the waterfront market in the morning. I did a couple of errands at Loulou's, with a farewell handshake from him, while Mieke was in the market, and we were under way at 1045. Everyone wanted to see Île Fourche, the small island three miles northwest of Baie Colombier, and we powered there in a very light breeze. It is sometimes called Five Fingers, because its separate, thinly steep hills of that number can be taken to look like a hand. Its one harbor cuts deeply into the island, right under the highest peak of about 300 feet.

Bill Eiman's guidebook for the area said to look out for a rock just above water, and a submerged reef right near it off the southwest point, and they were both plainly visible in a boil of surge. Steve, fidgety as usual, was dying to get on shore, and he swam in as soon as the hook was down, not bothering to wait for the dinghy, which Jim and Mieke took in for some beachcombing. The guidebook said that the island had no inhabitants but goats and very little vegetation, and it did look stark under the sun glare. There was also mention in the guidebook that the record for climbing the 300-foot peak was seven minutes—and there was Steve, charging up it like a marine on Iwo Jima as soon as he got ashore.

When he got back aboard, still breathing hard and wet from sweat and swimming, he claimed he had beaten the record by 30 seconds. Probably he was just antsy enough actually to have done it, but Jim gave me a raised eyebrow grimace behind Steve's back, so who knows. By now, Jim, who was the most easy-going, friendly guy imaginable, had gotten fed up enough with Steve to complain to me about him, completely unlike Jim's usual live-and-let-live attitude.

"I'm not going to clean up the head after that sloppy son of a bitch," Jim said. "He's an unbelievable slob."

I apologized for getting him into the situation and reminded him that it wouldn't last too much longer. He shrugged and said he would try to keep cool about it.

Our run to Philipsburg past the landmarks like Rocher Table, Petit Groupers, and Baril de Boeuf, lumps of rock sticking up, was under main and Flasher in, of all things, a light sou'wester, and we might have been in an America's Cup Race the way Steve twitched and fussed at the Flasher. I finally told him to take it easy, that it did not need tweaking and trimming every second, and got another fit of sulks as a reaction. I'm sure he felt he was stuck with a bunch of insensitive louts who did not know the fine points of sail trim, and he obviously had no concept whatsoever of the philosophy of cruising under sail as a relaxed way of enjoying nature. It should have been a beautiful sail, not a study in nervous fussing.

We anchored close to Bobby's, and Mieke went to work in the galley on her special Dutch dinner, refusing any help from Jane and seeming to be having a fine time. What she produced was a pear and cheese appetizer, sausage, mashed potatoes (which had never once before been produced on *Brunelle*'s stove), sauerkraut and bananas flambées. It was all hearty, spicy, and appetizing, and a distinct change from our usual fare, and we really enjoyed and appreciated it. It was a very nice way to say thank you. Steve, itchy as ever, decided to explore ashore, happily for the continuation of the good mood Mieke's meal had established, which we kept going with a concert of Benny Goodman tapes. Obviously, Steve was better off ashore and away from the old stick-in-the muds.

Mieke had arranged for a berth on a friend's boat and left us in the morning. We were very sorry to see her go. She was proof that all pier-head jumps are not risky, and she had been a charming shipmate. We lost touch with her after that, except for one gesture that seemed just like her. Back home in Rumson, we got a package of tulip bulbs from her in Holland at the proper planting time, as her final thank you for the days aboard *Brunelle*, and each spring as they bloom they remind us of her.

The weather reports, which are usually of little importance in this area except during the hurricane season, and which I claim could have been taped in 1957 and played almost daily since then, were talking of a trough over Hispaniola that might move on to the east, so I decided to wait a couple of days before heading across good old Anegada Passage again. One thing we did not need was another northwest wind for a westbound passage, unlikely as it would be at this time of year.

22

SOME SURPRISES

THERE WAS AN obvious question of why didn't I just kick Steve off the boat in St. Martin. I'll admit it was a tempting idea, but the story was that he had a plane ticket home from the BVI and was otherwise short of cash. It would have been a hardship to strand him in St. Martin, and I was, after all, responsible for those aboard my boat. I could have gotten in trouble for marooning someone who was without funds. Of course I could have bought him a ticket from St. Martin to the BVI, but I did not feel quite that generous, as I was already responsible for Jim Lillie's ticket and had not paid for it yet. So we decided to tough it out. Jim said he would do his best to live with the situation. Lately, Steve had not been quite as pesky and know-it-all about *Brunelle*'s shortcomings as a properly rigged ocean racer, finally aware, I guess, that he was getting nowhere with me on that subject, and maybe even realizing that there really was a difference between racing and cruising.

He was not the kind of guy I could have a heart-to-heart talk with, and I really was not interested in a basic remolding of his character. We just had a short-term adjustment to make, and we decided to do the best we could. It would have been nice, though, if there had been some redeeming feature we could point to. I hadn't found one yet, unless it was his eagerness to be physically involved, and it was too bad to have our winter adventures clouded by a sour note at the end.

With the Hispaniola trough still a factor, we decided to use the waiting time in some more cruising, rather than hanging around Philipsburg in the ever-present surge and constant barrage of noises from barking dogs, the squeal of automobile tires, the pealing of church bells from 0530 on, and the steady flow of jet planes into the airport. After some food shopping, we got under way in a light southerly, not so rare by this time of year, and eased around to Marigot on a smooth, pleasant sail. I always got a kick out of the panoply of luxury along St. Maarten's south coast, with the jet plane activity at the airport, and the array of fancy hotels standing tall in the sunshine. The last touch was the austere splendor of the low, white buildings of La Samanna resort at the western tip, beyond the French border. This is the most exclusive of all the resorts, with its own beautiful expanse of beach. It was pristine in its gleaming spread, except for the wreck of an old landing craft, a relatively rare type called an LSM, that had somehow become stranded just inside the western tip of the beach. I did not know its story, and its rusty bones were like a specter at the feast.

We anchored in Marigot in a gentle surge, rare here in tradewind weather, and I went ashore, depositing Steve in the process for his inevitable exploring, to make a dinner reservation at La Calanque for a "Captain's Dinner" to bid our seasonal farewell to these waters. Mieke said she would meet us there to make the crew complete, and it was a pleasant occasion, with even Steve on his best behavior and not too many complaints. Toasts and salutations went around the table, especially to Mieke in a final goodbye. Coquille St. Jacques and ris de veau were the choices, with a Blanc de Blanc wine at $14 (American money gladly accepted, as well as Visa or Amex). Marigot had become a sophisticated extension of France, in sharp contrast to the scruffy fishing village I had seen in 1958. Even this late in the season the restaurant, just across the waterfront "boulevard" from the harbor, had a good crowd.

Another "last visit" was to the boulangerie for their wonderful croissants for breakfast, with the usual French-English exchange between Madame and me, plus a loaf of French bread, redolently enticing, to take with us. We were hoping to head for the BVI that evening, and rather than wait in Marigot, we had a good sail around Anguillita and into Road Bay. It was one more chance for Steve to explore ashore (and get him off the boat for a few hours). The police station was closed, and the Gumbs had gone to Canada, so it was simply a matter of relaxing at anchor off the town dock until departure time for Anegada Passage. The trough over Hispaniola seemed to have dissipated. I would have been surprised if it had not, but it had been a good excuse for a couple more days of sailing in the area.

After all my ranting about the infamous treachery of Anegada Passage and its unpredictable changes of weather, this crossing was what might be called an anti-climax. We got under way at 1710 in a light easterly and settled into our two-hour wheel tricks, and it was easy enough sailing for Jane to produce stew for supper. We were on course 292°M, with staysail wung out, and sea conditions were moderate as we went our usual rolly way downwind. The partial cloudiness of a dark, moonless night produced some light rain at sunset, but the sky was glowing cheerfully up ahead, and there was no more wet. It was smooth sailing all night, with stars making peek-a-boo appearances between the clouds. I was on the 0400–0600 wheel trick when the skies started to lighten at 0425, with an unusual play of colors in the clouds, as the sunrise brightened. All shades of gold and red shot through them against open-sky patches of the most delicate blue, and the waves evolved from midnight black to deepest blue to the bright cobalt of day.

It was the friendliest encounter we had ever had with Anegada Passage, and there was Virgin Gorda (*not* St. Croix) looming up ahead as the day developed, welcoming us back. We swept inside Necker Island in the bright, new sunshine and hit the North Sound entrance buoys at 1110, 75 miles in exactly 17 hours, not a record-breaker by any means, but a respectable 4.5 knots of smooth sailing.

We made right for the Quarterdeck, and were charmingly greeted by Jenny, who put us next to *Alionora*. After lunch I took the launch to Gun Creek and Gafford Potter's taxi (we had the first of our many laughs over "bananas and cristofine") to Customs and Immigration at the airport. They made a fuss that there was a new rule that required all persons aboard to check in in person, but I finally talked them out of it, pleading ignorance, because of the transportation nuisance that would create, plus the fact we couldn't all get there before they closed. Then, for some reason, they took real exception to Steve's passport photo, I think because they had a policy of being careful about letting "hippies" in. Somehow, I finally got clear of them and got back to the boat after taking all afternoon. Roland and Lisa in *Klee* pulled into a nearby slip and came over for a drink at cocktail time and a catching-up session. They were about to start on an offshore passage to Maine (where we saw them that summer while on a cruise), but they were waiting out tropical storm Arlene, which had replaced the Hispaniola trough as a weather threat. It was over Cuba, headed northeast, rather early in the season (May 9th) for named storms.

Celebrating our return to the BVI with dinner at The Bitter End, we had another one of those reunions, this one with naval architect Bill Lapworth and his wife Peggy, with whom we had cruised in California. They were on a club cruise with a Los Angeles Yacht Club group. That the season had advanced was brought home to us by very warm sleeping that night, usually not a problem with *Brunelle*'s good hatch system, but the Quarterdeck, in the lee of the hill, can be relatively airless when the trades are light.

Steve heard that there was a Laser regatta in Bitter End in the morning, so we lazed and read while he worked off his competitive instinct by winning it. It seemed to make a new man of him, relaxed and satisfied. I guess poor old simple *Brunelle* had been too much of a strain for him.

There was yet another unexpected but expected reunion when Mort and Barbara Engel came in in their new Wellington 47, *Huntress*. I had sailed in the SORC several times with Mort and his partner, Jack Sutphen, in *J & B*, including the time of the widely publicized sinking of the sloop *Mary E* in the Miami–Nassau Race, when we rescued some of her crew. The Engels had settled happily into a cruising mode after many years of highly competitive racing, and it was good to catch up and compare notes.

On a beautiful afternoon, we had a fine sail under Flasher to Trellis Bay, and Steve was so happy with his Laser victory that he hardly tweaked the sail at all. It was great to settle into the familiar surroundings on an evening of lovely, clear sky and calm. Steve had reached the spot where his air ticket was good, and he left us in the morning. He hadn't cooked us a thank-you dinner, or, as a matter of fact, said a word of thanks, and parting was quick and easy. I went to the airport with him and reconfirmed our reservations. We had a couple more days to enjoy our Steve-less tranquillity, but the season was definitely winding down.

23

WRAPPING IT UP

WITHOUT STEVE, WE were in a thoroughly relaxed mood for finishing off our winter (and spring) in the sun, and were leisurely about making sail for an easy reach across Drake Channel, sparkling on a perfect day, for lunch at Cooper Island. It was quiet there, with just a couple of other boats in, and the young Limey bartender was so engrossed in reading *I, Claudius* that we had a hard time getting a drink out of him. I had a good seafood salad, but Jim and Jane said the mulligatawny soup was only so-so.

For our final sail of the season, it was a Flasher run across to Village Cay. Jim always got a kick out of the Flasher, as did we, and he was much better at setting and trimming it than twitchy, tweaky Steve. The many-colored vertical stripes above the collegiate and preppy horizontals seemed to shine with an extra brilliance on this afternoon of perfect Drake Channel conditions: pleasant trades on the quarter, the waves lively and blue under their whitecaps without being rough, and the sun lowering in the west casting its glow across us.

Probably it would have been better to have a sultry calm or rainsqualls for our last day, to make it easier to leave, but this was a sail to treasure, one to remember in the days ahead, and one to bring us back again for more of the same.

I radioed ahead to Village Cay to ask for a berth, and Joyce, the smiling local woman at the receptionist desk, who handled the VHF, came across warm and welcoming in assigning us to Slip 23, where *Brunelle* would hunker down for the summer. I still found it strange, by the way, to lay up a boat in May and commission it in November, even after several years of doing it.

Charlis, the dockmaster, was right there to wave us into our slip and take our lines, and he was interested, in welcoming us back, to hear that we had been to Antigua and back since we left him. It was Jim's last night, so we of course gave him "hashandpeas—" as a reminder of life in *Brunelle*. We were sorry to part with him, as he had been a perfect shipmate through thick, thin, and Steve over the past three years, and we could not have done what we did without him. But it was his last hurrah, as he was about to settle down to the humdrum task of making a living. We hoped he would have as good memories of us as we had of him.

Again, the sleeping was hot in contrast to the winter months of more breeze, and there was some rain during the night to give us a hatch drill. We had been going pretty hard and steadily for several weeks, and a good list of work items had been building. I did chores during the morning and got together with John Acland over summer dockage. By paying for the whole period in advance, we got a discount that made the monthly fee about $180. Peter Clarke showed up, and we went over a work list for him to take care of over the layup (his basic fee was $55 a month, with some labor charges extra).

The list went something like this: wax topsides, repair trailboard, repair hatch spring, repair door lock, lubricate roller furler and all winches, inspect rigging, replace worn gaskets on refrigerator lids, fix leaky faucet in after head, repair valve and leak in Avon, replace flag halyards, charge fire extinguishers, replace damaged shroud guards, provide sound insulation for engine hatch, arrange fumigation. Just the little things that pop up in the operation of a cruising boat.

Peter seemed undaunted by them, and I knew they would be done by the time we came back in November (maybe all in the last week, a feature of "island time" operation). I reminded him to remember where she was when he took *Brunelle* to Tortola Yacht Service for haul-out, and we had a beer to cap off the list and say goodbye. She was in good hands.

Looking ahead to the coming encounter with the San Juan airport on the way home, I was reminded of our hopes and expectations while we were fighting our way through there back in December, and I had to admit that, however high they were, they had been met. Of course there had been trials and tribulations of a sort (no names mentioned), but they had been minor compared with the tremendous pleasures and rewards. There had been the very real sense of shared experience and intimate contact with family and friends over a much longer and more concentrated time than could be managed in most normal encounters ashore. The ports and anchorages made a colorful Baedeker of memories, and what had seemed in advance like an aimless approach to day-to-day activities had turned into a great many accomplishments.

Best of all had been the hours of ideal sailing in an unmatched setting of sea, sun, and wind. That memory would carry us through a different kind of experience at home, where we thoroughly enjoyed summer daysailing in the seabreezes of the Shrewsbury River in our 18-foot catboat. The winter had been a time never to be forgotten, and we would always have the wonderful assurance that the golden memory could be lived again. We would be back.

Also from Sheridan House

Handbook of Offshore Cruising
by Jim Howard
Detailed, practical guidance on everything you
need to know about long-distance cruising.

Multihull Voyaging
by Tom Jones
A guide to short- and long-distance voyaging
that explains why multihull voyaging is
becoming more and more popular.

Sails Full and By
by Dom Degnon
A light-hearted tale of a circumnavigation
aboard a 41-foot ketch. Colorful places and people
encountered, from the crew to the locals.

Saga of a Wayward Sailor
by Tristan Jones
Tristan Jones' adventures aboard *Creswell*.
Jones survives storms, dismastings, smuggling,
being sunk by whales, and so on. Reissue of a
classic.

The Sailing Mystique
by Bill Robinson
A delightful collection of sailing stories which
the author has culled from a lifetime of writing
about boats and the sea.

America's Favorite Sailing Books